BECOMING PROSPEROUS

a beginner's guide

GILLIAN STOKES

A catalogue record for this title is available from the British Library.

ISBN 0 340 69773 3

First published 1997
Impression number 10 9 8   7 6   5 4   3 2   1
Year   2001 2000 1999 1998 1997

Typeset by Transet Limited, Coventry, England.
Printed in Great Britain for Hodder & Stoughton Educational, a division of Hodder Headline plc, 338 Euston Road, London NW1 3BH by Cox and Wyman Limited, Reading, Berks.

The author would like to thank
James Pollicott
for providing editorial assistance and
ideas for illustrations used in this book

To be truly rich, regardless of his fortune or lack of it, a man must live by his own values. If those values are not personally meaningful, then no amount of money gained can hide the emptiness of a life without them.

J Paul Getty, *How to be Rich,* 1966

Errors, like straws, upon the surface flow
He who would search for pearls must dive below.

John Dryden, (1631–1700) *All for Love Prologue*

CONTENTS

INTRODUCTION

Prosperity is an attractive proposition. You have picked up this book, so I know you agree with me. However, there are those for whom it has distasteful connotations. To admit to a desire for prosperity would seem the antithesis of a creative and socially caring person that they believe, or wish, themselves to be. I hope to encourage you to see that prosperity is a neutral concept; one that reflects a life lived with awareness, in harmony with one's personal situation and society. It is my aim to increase your sense of prosperity, which will in turn enrich your life.

Some people emphasise intellect at the expense of instincts, while others favour the creative at the expense of their intellect. This book suggests techniques to enhance and harmonise both aspects of the mind. Get the most from what you have by a deeper understanding of yourself. If you find that you want more, this book can help you to get it. It is not, however, my aim to give specific advice on savings, investments, retirement plans, or pay increases, because your course to gain prosperity will be absolutely unique to your situation, not a universal formula.

WHAT IS PROSPERITY ANYWAY?

Is prosperity something other people have? Not necessarily. Prosperity is the state of mind which you bring to endeavours, rather than the fickle and mysterious product of them. You may have already realised that you do not get a sense of prosperity from owning any particular set of status objects, nor from reaching any predefined level of income. Neither has prosperity anything to do with your position, relative to anyone else. If you think this way you are doomed to dissatisfaction, for no sooner do you gain reassurance of your status through the acquisition of one desirable object, than you decide another is essential. Any sense of triumph and well-being gained in this way is fleeting, because you have decided prosperity is a quality beyond yourself.

BUSHFIRES OF DOUBT

Too often we make the feeling of prosperity a commodity, a relative position, and link it to our ability to keep up with the latest fashion. Because this way of thinking locates the means of gaining satisfaction outside ourselves, never within, we will always find someone richer who stands between us and our sense of contentment. If we doubt our own qualities and worth relative to other people we create barriers to prosperity and success. If, on the other hand, we imagine prosperity as an energy or state of mind, we can make it ours to control and direct. If you realise how you have habitually closed off opportunities you can set about reversing the tendency, and replace it with confident action. As a result of reading

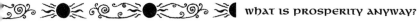

this book you will develop a more positive attitude and a better understanding of prosperity. Whether you find you feel prosperous with a lot or a little, a sense of prosperity is your birthright.

MONEY OR YOUR LIFE?

Wealth and success need not go hand in hand with negative traits. Many people confuse prosperity with its negative counterpart, greed, but this need not be true. Prosperity is merely the reflection of a life lived in harmony. When inner needs are monitored and acknowledged, and the outer situation has been thoroughly considered, appropriate action can follow. Prosperity is then the by-product of a good life, not the impossible goal of an unsatisfactory one.

A holistic approach to prosperity

How can you achieve prosperity, then? You need to bring creativity into money management. You must place yourself in a position to utilise such latent talents as engender a sense of prosperity. It is known that creativity involves both conscious and unconscious processes. Prosperity will, therefore, not be realised by thinking and planning alone, and certainly not by mere wanting. Action must follow if the creative process is to make any difference to your life. I will suggest how you can base your actions on well-researched foundations. Once you have developed a clear focus and positive attitude, you will be much better placed to recognise and evaluate opportunities. *Becoming Prosperous – a beginner's guide* offers a three-stage process for achieving this balance:

1   **Awareness of what you want**
    A process of reflection on your feelings concerning prosperity. Discovering your strengths and weaknesses. Relaxation and creative imagination techniques. What would you choose to be

doing in an ideal world? Why do you refuse prosperity now?
Learn from your intuition and dreams.

2 **Assessment of your situation**
Get to know your factual situation. What have you got to deal
with right now? What is available to you? What help can you call
on? How might you incorporate your talents and ideals into your
life? How do you find out more information about your interest?

3 **Action towards your goals**
Balance the creative and practical aspects of your nature. A
basis for effective action. Moving towards prosperity. Reviewing
the insights you have gained and assessing their practical worth.
Setting and achieving the goals you aspire to. Monitoring
progress and extending your goals.

Is prosperity guaranteed?

When your actions stem from a state of harmony between practical
considerations and a will which is focused on clear desires, yes,
prosperity is guaranteed. When you can invest any given situation
or action with personal meaning, the results will reward you with a
profound sense of harmony and well-being. If on some occasions
you find results are not exactly as you anticipated, or hoped, all is
not lost. Perhaps previously, you would interpret a setback as
confirmation that prosperity can never be yours; now you will be
equipped to see it differently. Instead of giving up your goals
completely, you will instead have the means to evaluate and learn
from the experience, and see it as merely information gathering on
your way to achieving the prosperity you deserve.

Whatever the outcome of your action, it will be just a part of the
dialogue between your inner needs and the world in which you live,
not a reflection of your ultimate worth. You will have a sense of
meaningful control. You are open to learn from life, and to gain
meaning from any event, rather than be crushed because you held too
rigid an idea of the necessary outcome. You will learn that bad things
can lead to good results, and prosperity can be found in the unexpected.

This change in outlook to a life of positive and holistic interactions, is infinitely more satisfying. It will sustain you in your next endeavour. Armed with additional knowledge, you use the setbacks to help you reach your goal, rather than let them feed the doubts that would have you give up. Anticipate what is before you so you can react to your best advantage whatever life brings you. Any blows you may sustain just serve to inform you of the nature of the challenge you face, and what you need to watch for in future.

Wbat do I need to start?

- A quiet time each day. At least twenty minutes without interruptions, if you can manage it. Make it known that you are unavailable at this time. Take the telephone off the hook and ignore the doorbell.
- A notepad or workbook and pen or pencil. You will build up a record of ideas which you can look back over, some of which will have a future relevance you cannot appreciate now. For this reason a book or file is preferable to scraps of paper.
- Access to information regarding current financial demands upon your income. What does it cost you to live as you do at present? What do you owe, and to whom? Can you identify likely future increases in demand, such as: children going to college, the end of entitlement to state benefits, health concerns, the forthcoming marriage of a child, essential but expensive vehicle repairs, urgently needed home maintenance?
- Details of your income from all sources at present. Details of known variations to this income expected in the year ahead. Include definite pay awards, investments or insurance policies that will mature, debt payments that are due to end.
- Imagination.
- Be willing to choose prosperity and to make such changes as become necessary, with due respect for your dependents.
- Confidence that you have a right to prosperity, or at least a willingness to discover that fact.

- Take advice wherever you can find it but evaluate its bias and relevance to you. Ask more than one expert. Use friends and family to vet ideas, as well as experts in your area of interest. Gather as much input as you can, but be aware of other agendas operating behind the criticism or negativity of those who know you personally. They may be less than sure of how your desire for change will affect them. Evaluate and discriminate between wise caution and a fear of change.
- Be open to learning from sources which you may have previously undervalued, such as your intuition and dreams or financial and career advisors.
- Start saving now. If you wait for the right time it never comes. Even if you still have debts to pay, start to save a regular amount now, however little. Practising deferred gratification will give you a sense of control and boost your self-esteem, as well as form a cushion against anxiety.

PRACTICE

1 Is prosperity the mark of a bad person?
2 What is the basic problem in believing prosperity is obtained from outside agents?
3 Can anyone become prosperous?
4 How many steps are there in the process to enhance your sense of prosperity?

PERCEPTION AND CONSCIOUSNESS

If the doors of perception were cleansed, everything would appear to man as it is, infinite.

William Blake (1757–1827)

So far we have taken a general look at prosperity and have considered why it may have eluded us. Before we go any further, I think it would be helpful to give some examples of how our perceptions and habitual ways of thinking influence and control the likely outcome of our actions. Once you realise this to be a fact, the practicality of the plan of action I propose will be apparent.

SENSE PERCEPTION: WHAT IS REAL?

As I have already suggested, how we perceive ourselves is of crucial importance to our perceived right to prosperity. How we see ourselves in relation to others, and our beliefs about our abilities and available choices influences results. As this is so important, I want to take some time to emphasise the fickle nature of perception and consciousness using everyday experiences.

There are those who believe that there is a real 'out there' which we can come to know: a world that is exactly the same for all of us, in which we exist as separate and different beings. By means of some

examples, I hope to show that it is not quite as simple as that. In truth, each of us creates our own individual world. We each bring the accumulation of our past experience to how we interpret what is out there, and to what we perceive and call 'real' in the present.

First, I will suggest examples using the medium of sight. It is possible, however, to furnish examples which beguile all the other senses: touch, taste, hearing, and smell; though not all can be conveyed by means of the printed page.

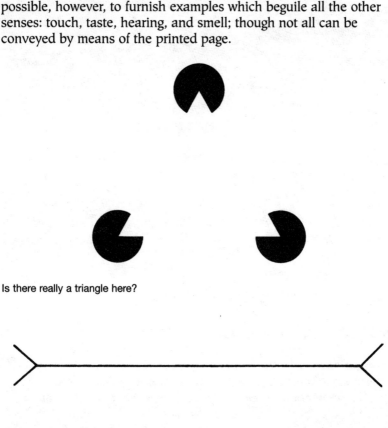

Is there really a triangle here?

Which line is longer? Neither, both are the same length.

Do you see two faces, or an urn?

I hope these illustrations serve to confirm the possibility of more than one interpretation of what you see. In two examples neither answer is right or wrong, in the other our eyes deceive us. It all depends on how your brain interprets lines on the page. Our perceptions of the real world can be similarly unreliable.

The 'real' world

We take for granted optical tricks played by our sense of perspective upon the relative size of objects in the landscape. If what we see truly mirrored reality, we would have to say that the moon was the size of a penny, and a distant church would fit into the palm of our hand. How can we be sure of what is real if things are not as they seem?

You may like to try an experiment which questions the certainty of touch. If you put one hand in a bowl of hot water and the other in a

bowl of cold water, then put both into a bowl of tepid water, the tepid water will feel warm to one hand and cool to the other. Both hands experience water you know to be of the same temperature yet your brain interprets the sensations from each hand differently according to prior experience.

Colour-blind individuals interpret the colours green and red in a different way from those who are not colour blind. Experiments also suggest that insects which have compound eyes, such as flies, see the world quite differently from humans, though because scientists do not have fly brains, they can never be sure what flies actually see. How far can we take the notion of the perceiver influencing what is perceived? Some philosophers have even speculated whether it is reasonable to suppose that objects exist at all once there is no one present to perceive them. What do you think? Would there be a sound when a leaf fell in the forest if there was no one there to hear it?

Do we all occupy the same world when our knowledge and beliefs about it differ and fluctuate so much? I hope I have established that perception depends in part on who, or what, is the perceiver, and you can now accept the possibility that we do not all experience an event in the same way. This fact has implications for your choice of poverty or prosperity. The scope for a variety of interpretations of a single event shows that we have a choice over the attitudes we hold. We must become aware of what they are and try to determine whether they are acting as a barrier to prosperity.

CONSCIOUSNESS – THE FILTER OF OUR PERCEPTIONS

The whole drift of my education goes to persuade me that the world of our present consciousness is only one of many worlds of consciousness that exist.

William James (1842–1910)

We have examined how interpretation of the outer world depends on the individual perceiver. This is even more true of what may be described as the inner world. Your state of consciousness affects how you think and act within the wider situation, although I agree much remains beyond your personal control. This influence has implications for your ability to experience prosperity.

Consciousness is not simply one of the properties of having a mind or brain, of being alive. Neither is it merely the simple difference between the states of wakefulness and sleep. Those are only two of the many forms that consciousness can take. Just as in sleep you may dream and thus enter a different state of consciousness, so there are numerous variations of what it is to be conscious when awake. Here are a few. You will doubtless be able to think of many more:

- Alert – maintaining a state of acute awareness.
- Daydreaming – fantasising; the mind in freefall.
- Introspection – examining your own emotions and thoughts.
- Certainty – holding a complete conviction of the truth.
- Attending – applying your mind.
- Concentrating – losing yourself in the focus of your interest.
- Noticing – placing a mental bookmark.
- Doubting – maintaining a sense of inner uncertainty.
- Reasoning – progressive thoughts on a theme.
- Observing – passively witnessing or watching carefully.
- Sensing – for example: pain, pleasure.
- Believing – maintaining faith or confidence in.

So, consciousness might be described as an inner event which arises from your personal interaction with your surroundings. It is not a fixed state. What is more, your interaction is constantly changing according to how you have learned to interpret what you perceive, and the shifting situation you are placed in. Consciousness is thus consciousness of 'something' with the 'something' varying according to the individual circumstances of the moment, and the perceptions of one particular person.

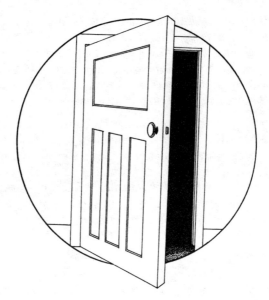

Is the door opening or closing?

Inner attitudes affect outer behaviour. As soon as we can say in any way that one person differs from another, we categorise. Stereotypical assumptions then influence our perceptions to some degree. This is not intrinsically a negative attribute. At its most basic it is part of the simple business of discerning one person from another, and discerning either person from the space which exists between them. All recognition depends on duality; there or not there. This natural state of discernment becomes slewed when differences are perceived as implying rigid characteristics which can be used to demean or enhance, according to the meanings we attach to them. Value judgements are added to the differences we perceive according to the assumptions we hold. These values will depend on what we have experienced or been taught, but difference itself need not automatically bear negative connotations. This is of great importance for realising prosperity because we select how we act in any given situation, according to our learned experience and cultural inheritance.

YOUR BIRTHRIGHT – choice denied?

Some of the influences that will shape a child's life, are in place even before it is born. If you doubt me, consider these:

- Our future parents, and society, place subtle differences in their expectations of us according to whether we are categorised as being of male or female gender. These expectations go largely unquestioned, and are culturally learned.
- Similarly, if we are born to a family with strong religious beliefs, certain rituals and requirements for our conduct will form part of our life experience, and in this area, specific behaviour will be mapped out for us. If these beliefs are strongly reinforced we will adopt, or reject, a particular moral code. We will have an attitude either way, and one that is different from a child born into another faith, or into a family with none.
- Race and nationality place another set of demands upon the yet-to-be born child, particularly if these collective ideas are important to the birth family, or ethnic group.
- Wealth, or lack of it, is another cause of a difference in the likely future life of our imaginary unborn child. Not only is the degree of educational opportunity and health care affected, but so too the set of acquired attitudes and tribal identity that goes with membership of a definable class.
- Siblings. If there are older brothers or sisters, some roles will already be taken within the family dynamic. By the laws of difference, there cannot be two children who are best or worst at any activity. Some options may, therefore, already be spoken for in the family's expectations.
- A first-born child, or a late addition to the family has quite different parenting. The first child may experience more of parental anxiety than the last does, and more expectation to be successful.
- Parents sometimes act out their own unfulfilled fantasies or ambitions through the lives of their children, by exerting strong pressure concerning education and the choice of career. A child

wishing to gain parental approval may attempt to oblige rather than fulfil personal ambitions. The concert pianist or doctor might be much happier in a different, or less exulted profession but feel unable to disappoint parental expectations, even long after their death.

These differences are examples of the endlessly varied world into which we are born. What is not predetermined, however, is how we choose to interpret the differences. Your chance to experience prosperity suffers when learned assumptions are rigidly adhered to without question as to their personal validity. As you will now realise, the beliefs you hold about your right and ability to enjoy a prosperous life, and whether you have a sense of personal satisfaction from what you do, together determine how likely it is you will attract and experience prosperity.

Ƌow can l change?

What each of us has learned and experienced, and how we have interpreted those events makes our perception unique. Fortunately for our chance of prosperity, we can choose how we respond if we find that our interpretations habitually place us at a disadvantage. The first step towards prosperity is to become aware of our learned response to it. It is said that some people see a cup as half full when others see the same object as half empty. Which are you, and why do you think that may be so? Do you believe you have a natural right to success? Are you happy with how you are in this respect?

I have tried to show that you create your own world, in the sense of how you experience life. No, you did not choose the circumstances of your birth, and perhaps no one would have freely chosen the knocks you have faced since then, but the point is, at any time you can choose to despair and be negative, or opt for the positive and change.

Personal awareness is a stepping stone to self-reliance and the ability to cope with change. If you do not take the time to get to know yourself, including your fears, it should come as no surprise

Is the cup half full, or half empty?

that you do not have the sense of prosperity that you aspire to. You must become receptive to who you really are, then with the factual information you take equal trouble to gather, you have the best chance of success in achieving your goals. Unfocused wanting simply will not do it. Prosperity is evidence of a harmonious life. It is as available to you as to someone with all the apparent advantages in society, if you learn how to focus your will and effort.

Remember, it is just as possible to be born with every apparent advantage, to have plenty of money, and yet feel wretched because there is no satisfaction in the life you are living. Prosperity is about more than cash and Cadillacs, though there is no reason why both of these should not be part of your prosperity if you want them. Some tramps die and leave millions, some millionaires act as though they were paupers. Attitude is all.

PRACTICE

1 Is there one version of reality that fits all?
2 Does my attitude affect my chances of experiencing prosperity?
3 Am I stuck with the attitudes that I have?
4 Wealth and prosperity can go hand in hand, so why is it that having wealth is no guarantee of feeling prosperous?

3 RESISTANCE TO PROSPERITY

The heart has its reasons which reason knows nothing of.

Blaise Pascall (1623–62), *Pensées*

I assume that you feel your prosperity might be improved because you are reading this book. It is, therefore, wise to consider reasons why you may be reluctant to risk change. It may seem to you that you must destroy in order to create, but what is required is only a controlled change.

If we have unacknowledged doubt about the morality of prosperity and our right to experience it, we may block the flow of our natural willpower. We may even interpret potential opportunities as difficulties or frightening challenges. If you carry a subconscious doubt of your value and worth, you have unwittingly created an inbuilt barrier to realising prosperity which limits effective action. After all, if you are not worthy, what right have you to the good life? If you blindly ignore your feelings and deny your fears, when you might free yourself by examining them, you are contributing to your own lack of prosperity.

FEAR OF THE UNKNOWN

When you allow yourself a quiet time of reflection, perhaps you will discover a fear of change so great, that you must respect it. If so, that is fine. You will at least be acting in conscious awareness of your choice to do otherwise. Maybe at another time you will feel

differently. We are not all adventurers and there are no right answers, only what is right for you. It is only prudent to avoid actions that are going to place you in a situation which makes you fearful or uncomfortable. However, if you become aware that fear of change is preventing you from becoming prosperous and you are not willing to settle for that, various opportunities are open to you.

Risk avoidance

You may recognise that it has been a pattern in your life to avoid taking risks and want to examine why that is so. Most often, behaviour of this kind can be traced back to childhood. As a child, you may have dealt with situations in which you felt strong emotions combined with a sense of powerlessness. By employing the reasonable tactic of not rocking the boat you felt safer. This is possibly a sensible option for a child or young adult, but is this tactic still serving you well?

You may decide that the time has come to take control and aim for prosperity, knowing that you will be taking all reasonable precautions. You are not asked to change from fear to recklessness. Failure or loss may occur, yes, but as an adult you realise that failure will not engulf you totally. You will still be here to try again.

Choosing what you have

Paradoxically, another way of resolving a fear of change comes when you realise that you wish to choose what you already have. You may find your present situation is tolerable even though previously you thought you wanted change. Perhaps you felt pressure to achieve more to please others. The people you wanted to please may no longer be with you, yet the wish to please them remained in you. Once freed from your obligation to those pressures you may be content and prosperous in your present situation. Be sure that you really are choosing the status quo, however. It could be an adult repetition of the childhood tendency to play safe, for fear of failure and embarrassment.

fear of success

Fear of change may represent fear of the unknown, of failure, or even of success. Does that sound crazy? Just consider a minute. To become successful and prosperous might involve a considerable reappraisal of who you are. Anyone who risks becoming visible may have rocks thrown at them. You may discover you have a greater need to be popular and liked, than to be prosperous and successful. Of course, if you decide to be prosperous, successful *and* ethical, you could have it all. There is no rule that says you must become mean and ruthless to get on. Consider then, whether an inability to allow yourself prosperity is in fact a fear of success. Remember that prosperity arises from a state of harmony. You may be fearing that success will involve you in a set of problems that will leave you feeling ill at ease and out of your depth.

Nasty money

Maybe during your reflections you discover to your surprise that you have a deep seated distaste for money, and an assumption that prosperity and money are indivisible. As I have said previously, prosperity is not an automatic property of the rich. There have been many cases of extremely wealthy, famous and powerful people who continued to hold fears which prevented them from realising the harmony of prosperity. Likewise there are tramps and Buddhist monks with scarcely any material possessions, who feel prosperous. It is not about what you have relative to others, it is about how you feel about what you have, and what you do with your life.

Money versus spirituality?

It is possible for you to aspire to selflessness while denying, even to yourself, your hankering for the material life. If that is the case you may find any activity designed to increase prosperity as suspect.

You will resist and feel ashamed of those aspects of yourself whenever they surface. Be assured, you will be most unlikely to succeed until you resolve this conflict. Remember, material wealth is not of itself a bar to spirituality. You could become a great benefactor for humanity if you use your creativity to the full and as a result become prosperous and wealthy. Accept that money and artifacts are just representations of energy, and it is you who decides on their meaning and use.

Ḏarⲙony

Prosperity is about harmony. You are not asked to push yourself far from your comfort zone, but you are asked to become aware of what motivates the choices you make. To find out how best to focus your will on prosperity you must establish what you truly desire, as well as what feelings have prevented you from achieving it. Most of us get entangled in the complicated web of an unplanned life, one in which much of what we do is determined by circumstance and duty. As a result, the ability to get in touch with our own needs becomes neglected. The energy we must use to deny what we dream of, is energy no longer available for what we actually do. Small wonder then if prosperity is lacking.

We all spend much of our lives in a semi-automatic trance. We fulfil the demands that our situation and upbringing make on us, and along the way satisfy as many of our own urges as circumstances, our sense of who we are, and the law, permit. As nothing can be created which has not been first brought to mind, allow time for positive daydreams and aspirations. I shall discuss how to do this in a later chapter.

pRACTICE

1 How do we cut ourselves off from a sense of prosperity?
2 Must you become mean and selfish to become prosperous?
3 Are wealth and a concern for others incompatible?
4 Are rich people automatically prosperous too?

4

SELF-AWARENESS AND PROSPERITY

Perfect freedom is reserved for the man who lives by his own work, and in that work does what he wants to do.

R. G. Collingwood (1889–1943), *Speculum mentis*

*A*t the risk of stating the obvious, to feel prosperous you must know *what it is you want. Before you can focus your energies and efforts productively, you must take some time to know yourself honestly. If encouraged, your imagination and intuition can prompt the directions that will bring you to a sense of prosperity. You must ascertain your aims and desires, and how much effort you are prepared to put into realising them. You also need to examine why you are not experiencing prosperity now.*

Do you buy things to make you feel better about a job you are too afraid to change? Do you see the size of your salary as proof of your value? These days it is unwise to assume your current financial status is permanent. Would you continue to feel valuable if you no longer had your job, or present income? In this chapter we will look at ways to know yourself better so that you focus your energies appropriately.

GETTING TO KNOW YOU

Not to know something is a great part of wisdom.

Hugo Grotius (1583–1645), *Docta Ignorantia*

If you have been in the habit of coping with life by fielding whatever it threw at you, you may have lost touch with what you really want, and what your real talents are. You may have felt you had to compromise; to get along with this boss, to cope with being in this family, or from this neighbourhood. However, there is a part within us that never compromised. Intuition has access to this core of personal truth which can be incorporated into the life we live, and inform the choices we make for our future.

It is important to allow some space for the unexpected. You cannot fill a cup that is already full, so do not make the mistake of trying to prejudge or plan down to the last detail. Rationalising has its place, but is greatly enhanced by allowing your unconscious to surprise you. You gain a considerable advantage in all activities when you marry your intuition to your practical expertise. Armed with the knowledge of what you might be doing in an ideal world, plus the knowledge of your actual situation in this one, you will be in the best position to formulate a set of realisable goals for fulfilling personally important aims.

WHY BOTHER WITH HUNCHES AND INTUITION?

Many creative and innovative geniuses, from Archimedes to Pasteur and Einstein, experienced problems which their rational thought had failed to solve. In each case it was a flash of insight which lead to the solutions for which they are now famous. Admittedly, they probably would not have recognised the worth of their insights unless they already knew the details of the problem at hand. What insight provided in each case, was the intuition of how the

21

Einstein's breakthrough

information already observed, but not yet recognised, could be meaningfully interpreted.

You may have had similar experiences. For instance, have you ever had a lapse of memory, of someone's name or telephone number for instance, despite every effort to recall it? Only when you stop trying to remember and release your mind to freewheel, does the name or number suddenly come to you, perhaps when thinking of something else entirely. Similarly, crossword puzzle fans will know how the mind will sometimes provide the answer to a clue only when you stop trying to work it out, and move on to consider another clue. If you reflect on your past successes, you may realise that intuition was involved to some degree. There is a sense of rightness when inspiration strikes. It seems to make sense of loose ends. I have come to trust and respect this feeling.

It seems we are not nearly as clever as we think we are, or more accurately, it is not purely thinking that makes us clever. A solid groundwork of knowledge and effort is important, but alone, not enough. Once you realise you have the ability to tap your

unconscious, and can recognise and trust intuition, it can be a useful tactic to employ quite deliberately, as another aspect of your intelligence. Having set the agenda by fruitless effort to think a problem through, if you quiet your mind an answer will appear when you least expect it. The more habitually you still your mind, the more often your intuitions will have a bearing on the questions you hold within you at the time. You will find valuable insights flow when your mind gets used to being listened to at last. This can be of lifelong benefit for so long as you make your conscious mind available. I am not suggesting you will experience an audible voice, in the style of Joan of Arc, though I would not prejudge how insight may come to you. In my case, I think of it as an *aha!* moment. There is a different quality to that of thinking or wishing. The intuitive idea seems to present itself complete and out of the blue.

Negative ideas and intuition

True intuition seems to come from a higher wisdom within us, in that it never prompts unethical actions. If you feel prompted to act in any way that would hurt others, what you are experiencing arises from ego desires or repression, not from insight or intuition. Any such thoughts should be distrusted and disregarded. If negative suggestions persist it would be helpful to seek some counselling from a professional source, because you need to clear up whatever the underlying difficulty is before you can proceed towards your positive goals. A good counsellor should be like a tourist guide who can lead you through unfamiliar country, but who will take you to visit only the places you choose to visit.

Science and intuition

Rational thinking, associated with use of the left hemisphere of the brain, seems to use serial processing and employs language. To put it another way, when we think we use the same concepts as when we speak. The intuitive mind however, seems to function by parallel processing. It operates from the non-verbal basis associated with use

of the right hemisphere of the brain. This involves the use of free associations rather than serial ones, which enables us to see a problem in a completely new light. The right hemisphere of the brain makes connections not immediately apparent to your usual, linear way of thinking. It often uses symbolic imagery more like that of dreams.

We should view imagination as an additional resource, not as a nonsensical failing. If rational thinking had been capable of making the connections we seek there would be no need to ask for insight. Respect your dreams and intuition. You can come to know your personal symbolism as well as you do your spoken language. By means of relaxation techniques and creative imagination, your wants and desires will surface and you will come to know yourself better. This has nothing to do with daydreaming about winning a fortune. With practice, and the techniques I suggest, you will empower your full potential, even if it is buried beneath layers of social and parental conditioning.

CREATIVE RELAXATION

Pick a time when you can settle down and allow your mind to relax, and your thoughts to wander uninterrupted. You will need at least twenty minutes, or if you can manage it, more. Make this a daily addition to your routine if you can, but however frequently you can make time available, do make it a new habit. Consider it as mental hygiene, which you would not leave undone any more than your bodily hygiene. You will not regret the commitment, and your prosperity depends upon it.

It is a good idea to keep a notepad nearby at all times when you begin this process. Once started, quite often the insights come to mind when you are distracted by a mundane activity such as washing up, jogging, ironing, or fixing the car. I often have my best ideas just when I am ready to sleep, or on waking. As I keep a pad and pencil by the bed it is no hardship to jot them down. If I had to leave my warm bed in search of pen and paper I probably would not

bother, and would then lose the ideas. In this way, I record the insights and still get another half hour's snooze before getting up.

ḣow ḋo ɩ ʙeɢɩɴ?

Make yourself comfortable. Whether you sit or lie down is up to you. If you find it more relaxing to have pleasant scent in the air, or to sit by candlelight, do so, but no props are necessary. Indeed, if you are to keep to this routine wherever you are in the world, you may find that acquiring a dependence on props creates a hindrance. If you sit, do so in whatever way you will be able to relax. It will not help if your body is telling you about this twinge and that ache all the time. The lotus position is not required, neither is it forbidden. At first you may find that you fall asleep when you intend to still your mind, especially if you lie down, but if you make the commitment to return to this relaxation every day, eventually you will not sleep. Your mind will recognise your commitment and co-operate.

Do not allow thoughts of your daily reality to occupy your mind while relaxing, because anxieties and habitual thinking will confuse you. Consideration of your present situation will be added to what you discover at a later point. Nevertheless, before you become practised at stilling your mind you will probably find the thoughts that occur will be a form of everyday mindstuff. These thoughts are like radio static before you have tuned in to the radio station you want. Be patient. You are unlikely to have useful ideas flooding into your mind at the first attempt, so persevere. If you had been habitually ignored by someone, you might not trust sudden overtures either. Your intuition is no different. Persistence will increase the efficiency of your creative mind.

ṁeɴtaʟ cḣatteʀ

If you are getting pointless thoughts rattling around, do not try to force them out. Just accept each as it occurs. Note it inwardly, and let it go. It might help to imagine these thoughts as written on pieces

of paper which you place in a pending tray. Reassured that they will be dealt with eventually, the thoughts should go quietly in this way. Use whatever image works for you to clear and calm your mind again. Here are some ideas you may find helpful to still the chatter.

- Picture an empty room, painted in a restful colour. Ask any thoughts that enter the room to go to the waiting room along the hall, where they will be attended to soon.
- Picture a clear desktop. Any thoughts that appear can be placed in the filing tray for later. Keep the desk clear.
- Picture a long, empty beach. Wander along it and hear the tide lapping. Send any chattering thoughts out to sea. They will be picked up by a boat later.
- Imagine you are watching a large, blank television screen with a feeling of peace and calm. Tune out any images that enter the blank screen.

By definition it is impossible to relax by struggling. Acceptance is more useful than becoming tense, or stressed about the quality of your thoughts. Eventually this chatter will abate and frenetic thoughts will subside. Once you have achieved a state of equilibrium, stay with it. Do not particularly note that you have arrived somewhere, because that would be another thought, and in having it, you will have lost what you sought to note. There is nothing you have to do, or expect. For a while, just be. Allow yourself to float mindlessly, just as you would do with your body in order to float in the sea or a swimming pool. Your problems will still be there to come back to later. They do not need your attention right now.

TRUST

If you allow your body to become tense or you panic when floating in water, you lose your balance and sink. The only way to float on water is to lie back, breathe, and trust that the water will hold you up. A calm, relaxed mind requires similar trust. An example of what I mean is the difference between the mental effort of a learner driver, who actively tries to process every piece of information consciously

in an anxious attempt at full control, and the alert but more relaxed mental state of the experienced driver, who knows he or she can entrust some information to already learned responses. Learning to ride a bicycle and then knowing how, is another example of these different states of mind.

When you have remained in a relaxed state for a while you find thoughts of a different kind occur. They may seem to have no relevance, but just watch and listen without judgement. At the end of your session, you should note down these thoughts, however weird and silly you may initially think them. Do not worry if you have no thoughts or images that you can recall. If you have stilled your mind, you will have set the process of insight going, regardless of whether messages are immediately returned to your rational mind.

Ask within

After a period of quiet calm, with or without insights, you are ready to gently consider a specific question to which you want an answer. When I say consider, I do not mean that you snap back into your usual, waking, problem-solving mode. Since prosperity is the issue at hand, I will use that example, but the means would be the same for any topic.

Once your mind is relaxed, allow one thought to enter and remain. How you do this depends on your chosen way of stilling your thoughts.

- If you used the television screen image, imagine this one idea now appears on your screen, perhaps in words, perhaps as an image. You can adjust the set to improve the picture or sound quality.
- If you pictured yourself on the beach, now imagine sitting or lying on the sand while daydreaming this question. You see it clearly in your mind's eye.
- If you used the idea of the clear room or desktop, this one item appears now in some tangible form, and is allowed to remain.

Introducing a topic for meditative thought is an allowing process, and should not involve effort, so do not steer the thoughts you think ought to be connected to the question. If your mind wanders completely off the point, just gently return to the specific that you had decided on. Gently hold your question, and wait. Be with the idea in the stillness for a while. Thoughts will rise and sink. Mentally note them, but do not cling to them. If you can write them down without losing your relaxed state, do so. If a stream of thoughts occurs, gently follow them as an interested witness rather than as creator. Wrong thinking can prove to be right thinking so do not be prejudiced. You have come to learn, not to direct.

Introduce prosperity

If you decide that having a lot of money is your goal, you would now need to find what specific qualities you have; what talents, if encouraged, might lead to success and the money you seek. Imagining yourself rich without the how, would not work because it is an abstract idea. To focus on specifics is all important.

Everyone has a gift. It may not be obvious that you do if you are in the habit of putting yourself down. Are you methodical, imaginative, creative or loyal? Maybe you have a way with animals, the elderly, or children? Can you draw, or do you have a fine sense of colour? Are you gifted with mathematics, or music, or languages? Do you find it easy to mix with people? Are you good with your hands? Do you have a knack for judging spacial measurements; a good sense of balance or a fine voice, perhaps? Are you great at ideas even if not so hot at realising them, or maybe you are great at realising goals if someone else sets them? Everyone has special qualities. You may not appreciate what they are if they are not currently being recognised as a specific job title in the market place. If identified, your talents may be seen as of great benefit to employers, or can form the basis of branching out on your own. If no one else is selling the talent you have to offer this may be the moment to do just that.

FIND YOUR TALENTS

Allow yourself total freedom of choice concerning what you would wish for yourself. Do not allow the limitations that you presently believe to be insurmountable to bar the free flow of your imagination. Responsibilities and practicalities will be considered after the creative imagination has offered its new pathways to you. The possibilities for talent are endless once you think beyond set job titles which is why there are no universal answers to prosperity. No two people will have the same talent, ambition and energy in identical combination. The following are some suggestions to get you going with specific questions. Each could make a separate session. You can and should also create your own.

- What would give me a sense of prosperity?
- What would I be doing if I had none of the limitations that I feel prevent my prosperity now?
- What particular talent do I possess? (This may not be a talent you currently use in any way, but you know it to be your especial gift.)
- Which sense: vision, hearing, touch, smell, or taste, do I operate best with? Consider the type of work which requires the use of that sense.
- How would I feel if I were wealthy?
- Do I deserve to be prosperous?
- Am I content with the direction my life is taking at the moment?
- What work does my natural talent best fit me for? (Regardless of imagined practical limitations at present. Consider as many variants as occur to you.)
- Do I believe that money is the root of all evil?
- Do I believe that I am not prosperous because I do not deserve to be?
- If I give of myself or my money, do I do so with love or a sense of loss?
- Do I begrudge giving?
- Does my current lifestyle allow me to use my creativity? (Creativity in the broadest sense, not limited to artistic creativity. Even tax collecting can be creatively approached.)

- To become prosperous, must I sell my soul?
- Does prosperity mean that life must be unpleasant and difficult?
- Do I believe that to want prosperity is shameful?
- Is it wrong to spend?

You will not get a clear response if you present your intuition with a garbled list, so take at most, one or two related thoughts at a time. Some of the suggested questions are intended to reveal your attitude to prosperity, and perhaps reveal why you avoid it. It may be that you need encouragement to spend money rather than to earn it. Perhaps you have such a fear of loss that it is difficult to trust that you can remain prosperous while spending or giving. Your response to basic questions such as these will help to determine which specific questions you then move on to ask in another session.

Patience is essential. Think of this as tuning in your radio receiver. Make your reception as clear as you can and then wait for the broadcast. You are likely to have to ask several questions to cover all the aspects that you need to know, which may take several sessions. For instance, once you have an idea of your particular gifts, and I do assure you everyone has some, you would then need to ask what range of opportunities there are for exercising this talent.

fermentation

You must allow time after each session before attempting the next, because your intuition will not always give answers during the quiet period. Insights may come when driving, washing up, or during any familiar and routine activity when the mind is not actively making conscious effort. You may find that you start to have vivid dreams, perhaps for the first time. Record these. They may not immediately make sense to you, but could well contain your answers in symbolic form. Your daily relaxation routine allows you to steadily harvest the elements of a complex enquiry. Discovering your desires may also bring up all the reasons why you resist prosperity, so make a note of

these feelings too, if you experience them, because you will need to explore them later. Keep your notepad or journal to hand to note any answers and ideas you come up with. You may believe you could not forget, but if your dream is not recorded you risk losing some, or all of the intuitive treasure you have been given, once your stilled mind is busy again.

It is important to be honest with yourself. You will have to put your will and energy to work on what you discover, if you want to gain a sense of prosperity. You may settle for self deception, and participate less than wholeheartedly, and then fail to become prosperous, but know that will be because it is what you have chosen.

The creative prosperity checklist

1 Prepare the ground
- Discover the questions appropriate to *you*. Practise self-awareness techniques.
- Focus your logical mind on the facts. Think through all the aspects of the issue as far as you know them.

2 Freewheeling
- Stop actively considering the issue. Give your unconscious the green light to get to work. Free your mind from preconceptions of what the answer will be, and how it should present itself. Allow a fermentation of ideas without directing your thoughts.

3 Insight
- Experience the intuitive moment: an unexpected flash of inspiration. This may be a solution, a partial answer, or a more helpful rephrasing of your problem, and can occur at any time or place, but will not happen if consciously thinking about the issue. Free the channels to receive rather than transmit.

- Experience an intense sense of satisfaction and pleasure along with this new-found clarity of thought. The sense of rightness which accompanies an intuitive solution is one indication of its being a genuine insight.

4 Check the practicalities
- Return to using your rational, logical mind. Research whether your insight really is valid.
- Apply the new insight, if valid, to your original material and consider its worth for you. If practicable, set about implementing the new idea now. Seize the moment. If you cannot, give consideration to a definite timetable for its implementation in the future.
- If you gain insight which solves only a part of the problem, restart the process, but from this new vantage point. Go on adding insight in this way, in incremental steps towards your ultimate goal.

PRACTICE

1 Everyone has talents which can be exploited, even you. True or false?
2 Which famous discoverers of scientific truths benefited from intuitional insights when their rational thinking failed?
3 How can wrong thinking prove to be right thinking?
4 What are the four main steps on the creative prosperity checklist?

AWARENESS THROUGH DREAMS

Dreams function by means of the holistic, parallel sifting of experience. The messages within dreams are rarely verbal, or consecutive. They present their material to us in a symbolic, visual form, unlimited by the linear time constraints of our waking life and the limitations of the material world. Freed in this way, connections are made and scenes depicted which would be impossible in everyday life. This does not mean that they depict nonsense, however. Their different approach to sifting information offers the means to understanding that rational thinking may overlook.

The different way that dreams process information makes it less likely that our conscious, linear, habitual, thought patterns and presumptions will interfere and override. Dreams can, therefore, be a useful route for insight, if you learn to decode them. By means of the kaleidoscopic scenes and images of dreams, your unconscious presents meaning for your conscious mind to understand, if it will. All the elements of a dream represent aspects of yourself. As a result, a dream can offer you priceless information not otherwise available.

What if I do not dream?

You may believe you do not dream, but scientists have discovered that we all spend a part of our sleep in the dreaming state. Where some people differ is in their ability to recall what has been dreamed. I can promise that if you diligently open your mind to the

relaxation exercises and show willing, in the sense of a ready notepad and pen by the bed, you will start to recall dreams. As with insight gained through stilling the mind, you have only to show willing by practice and intent.

Dreams can seem to be complete rubbish until you take the time to examine them for their symbolic sense. Some will, indeed, be merely a reworking of elements of the immediate past, but not all. Once the dream habit is initiated you can ask a specific question as your last thought before sleep, and often get the answer you seek. It is only the answers which resonate as true to you which are correct, however, not those of any book, though these may be helpful if you are completely at a loss to understand an image you wish to decode. Once you record and work on your dreams regularly, you will find certain symbols recur, and become a visual shorthand. Your task then becomes faster and more accurate as you learn the signposts in this strange territory.

Interpreting Dreams

To establish your own interpretations, ask yourself what a dream image means to you. The answer you get is more likely to be the right explanation for you, rather than any entry in a dream dictionary. This is because the dream dips into your memories and experiences for its references, and you may have reasons for a unique association with a particular item. Ask yourself what is the first thought you associate with each item or person in the dream. Do this with all elements of the dream, both animate and inanimate. You can even include the weather, items of furniture, money, plants … whatever was in the dream. If a dream recurs it is emphasising a topic you still have not dealt with consciously yet. This may require only that you acknowledge a situation, rather than act.

If no particular association springs to mind, see if a good dream dictionary can help you by suggesting an interpretation, but if the definition does not seem appropriate, do not assume the book is necessarily correct. Your dream symbols may not fit any generalisation and you may find different books interpret the same

symbol quite differently. However, a dream dictionary is useful to get you started. It can suggest commonly held interpretations of certain symbols, in this and other cultures. (See 'Further Reading'.)

When analysing a dream, pay particular attention to the aspect that seemed most important. Often that will be the last image before you awakened, or the aspect which evoked the strongest emotional response. If you know that there was more to a dream but you forgot it, do not worry. It is probable that the lost information was not vital or you are not ready to understand it. If it was important it will represent itself in a different dream at another time. This is also true if you fail to understand the meaning of an important dream message, even though you do recall it.

BIG DREAMS

Some dreams have a numinous quality; a sense of specialness which you cannot explain, but can recognise when compared with others. These are particularly important dreams to work with. You will know one if you have such a dream, without a doubt. You may find that scenes in a *big* dream foretell events yet to come, perhaps years off.

When you record all your dreams you will be able to confirm that events were known to your unconscious mind, maybe years ahead of conscious reality. *Big* dreams are also very helpful if you wonder whether you are taking the right course of action. To see yourself doing what you most wish to do, can encourage you to redouble your efforts, so that the dream does indeed presage future reality. It can give you the courage to believe what you desire is somehow meant to be, if you see it in a dream.

BAD DREAMS

As with waking intuitions, negative or frightening images are not to be taken literally. Dreams of a death, for example, are to be

interpreted as a positive harbinger of change, for in order for a new experience to occur, something must give way. All change is thus a death, and this is all the dream suggests. Dreams do not foretell an actual death in 99.9 per cent of cases.

To dream of violence can be an indication of how strongly you want to change a situation, and is not to be taken as an invitation to act out the violence. It may be that you are experiencing anger or frustration through the medium of the dream, which is then a healthier outlet than if you enacted it awake. If you see yourself attacked in a dream it may reflect a real life situation of unresolved conflict. It does not foretell real violence against you.

By presenting an image you associate with a particular emotional tone, a dream conveys information you may have been unable or unwilling to accept consciously as yet, such as your feelings of anger or frustration about a situation. Maybe in waking life your sense of duty overrides your personal feelings. The dream is reminding you that you are less serene under the surface. Acknowledging the honesty of your emotions can go a long way to neutralising harmful effects which may otherwise leak out, as when we misplace anger on to a less powerful person, because we are too afraid to acknowledge the resentment felt towards a person whom *you* feel powerless before.

Over time you will get to understand your personal dream language. The symbols convey meaning according to your personal experiences, plus what you have learned of collective and cultural experiences. Perhaps a specific example would help you to understand the nature of symbolic prompting available through a dream:

Dream example

A dreamer witnessed a funeral procession in which a coffin was being carried by hooded figures, like monks or nuns. Following behind, the dreamer entered a church and noticed with particular attention, a 50 pence coin on the floor in the doorway. Stepping over this, the dreamer took a seat in the church. The funeral procession disappeared as it crossed the threshold. Looking around, the dreamer recalled all the

other persons present from childhood: faces now seen vividly which
could no longer be called to mind in the waking state. Surprised to see
and remember these people, the dreamer now noted a table, on which
were examples of a hobby successfully enjoyed during schooldays.
Sensing that the teacher was about to come in and praise the dreamer's
work, which was on top of the pile, the dreamer re-experienced feelings
of pleasure, pride and self-denying embarrassment as was the case in
childhood when singled out for praise. The dream ended.

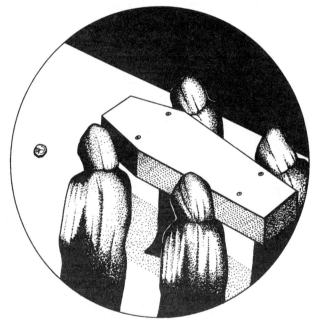

Dream example

The INTERPRETATION

The dreamer was to become 50 years of age in the following year.
Such a birthday was perceived as a threshold moment, and a time
for evaluating life so far. Following the funeral with its robed
pallbearers meant it was time for old habits to die, as depicted
symbolically by the pun of religious robes, or habits. The feelings in

the church mirrored those the dreamer used to experience at school when praised by a teacher for work done. Fearful that praise would cause alienation from friends, the child chose to repress and belittle the hobby, and continued to do so well into adulthood. There remained, however, a secret desire to practise it some day. This dream was clearly saying that the time had come to break the habit of self-denigration, and cross the threshold to reclaim that forgotten skill. The age of 50 would prove to be a threshold for honouring a talent of great personal importance which led to increased prosperity for the dreamer.

Synchronicity

Interestingly, life presented the dreamer in our example with another nudge on this theme. It was some months after the dream that a 50 pence coin literally dropped out of the sky. This was so startling that it immediately brought the dream back to mind and emphasised the deep importance of its message. Until this bizarre reminder, the hobby had been ignored again. Now the dreamer realised how personally important it was to admit to the talent and exercise it.

Rationally, one may say a bird such as a magpie or jackdaw dropped the coin, as was probably the case. Readers familiar with the work of psychologist Carl Jung will know, however, that synchronicity such as this occurs and can effect tangible objects, if powerful forces of the mind have been awakened. Jung cited several examples of similarly bizarre coincidences which served to jolt clients' attention. The unconscious thus can, and does, affect the conscious. There is, therefore, every sense in respecting dreams.

PRACTICE

1 Why should you pay attention to dreams?
2 Do bad dreams necessarily lead to bad events?
3 How can you choose what subject you dream of?
4 Does a dream symbol have the same meaning for everyone?

6
ASSESS YOUR
PRACTICAL
SITUATION

In the field of observation, chance only favours those who have been prepared for it.

Louis Pasteur, 1911

We have tackled the thought patterns, now to the practicalities. There is no sense in skimping this aspect, even if you find the thought of sorting out your affairs is daunting. If you lack a sense of prosperity now, nothing less than a thorough overhaul of your situation will improve your quality of life. Cheat on the thoroughness and you cheat on yourself.

Maybe you find creative activities more to your taste than practical ones. Who decreed the practical should never be creative? You probably already use these skills. Do you organise your life to accommodate employment and family; friends; sports and hobbies? Then you already have the necessary talents. You know how to find out where these activities take place, you solve transport and finance requirements, and generally juggle the logistics of multi-tasking some or all, at once. Use those creative talents on prosperity now.

Overcome reluctance to taking responsibility for your position. If it seems an indulgence to focus on yourself you are mistaken. It is an act of social responsibility, because a prosperous life is a contented life, with more to offer others: of your self and of your resources.

Evaluate your skills

If the exercises in self-awareness revealed a sense of prosperity for you involving a particular type of employment, now is the point at which to think about whether you have the necessary skills, and if not, what is involved in getting them. Use your notebook to jot down your thoughts freely.

- What are the activities that you accomplish with greatest ease?
- Which activities bring you most satisfaction?
- Is there a unifying quality of experience about these activities?
- Do you get greater enjoyment when working with your hands rather than your head, regardless of the nature of your present occupation?
- Write down what should be in your life to make you feel prosperous.
- Make a list of the problems preventing your prosperity.
- What do you most value about your life now, and what least? Can you think of ways to increase the former and diminish the latter?
- Do you favour your intellect over your intuition, or your intuition over your intellect? Do you habitually approach a problem with a bias towards one mode or the other? Consider what past influences encouraged this attitude. Are you willing to try a different approach?
- Do you find you have under-used intellectual capacity? Perhaps this is revealed in your fondness for cryptic crossword puzzles, or games of strategy, like chess, or your ease with mental arithmetic, foreign languages, or a hobby designing computer games?

Watch what you do in everyday life and note how you feel doing it for a few weeks. The monitoring over time is necessary because any armchair appraisal would produce only the beliefs you have acquired about yourself, rather than the actual talents you are blessed with – yes, blessed with. Everyone can find some quality that brings them joy, and for which they have an aptitude. It may be unlike anyone else that you know, and may conflict with the prevailing view of who and what you are, but it should be cherished by you. 'Wrong thinking' can be right thinking.

PROSPERITY JOURNAL

Make a note of what you believe your talents are. It is helpful to keep a journal, for this and the other practical aspects of prosperity planning. The act of writing ideas down helps to make them more real and certain to you. Do not be shy of others reading your workbook, you will always keep it to yourself unless you choose otherwise. I find that ideas frequently flow years ahead of the external circumstances that will enable me to enact them, most especially from dreams. It is then fascinating to look back and see where the seed thought was planted all those months or years before. You may later need the ideas you jotted down years before, so do not be too hasty in destroying them.

List all the aspects of a proposed change, as you see them. Put down points for and against. Do not worry if at the start you have not crystallised the exact nature of the changes you want to make. If you have only a vague sense of the subject area that you are interested in, doodle on your notebook. Your unconscious may help you out once you overcome inertia. Put down as many variants as you can come up with which touch upon the subject to some extent. Brainstorm connections that you associate with your talent or interest. Try radically changing your preconceptions of what scope exists for it. What is the essence of your talent or interest, freed from these preconceptions? Think laterally. Chop the tree down so that you can benefit from the new shoots that emerge.

This is your dialogue with yourself. Be honest. This is not the forum where you need care at all what others would think of your writing. They will not see it unless you choose to share it. Cheat on your observations and you undermine your efforts. Do you really want prosperity, or is the thought of such a change intimidating? Do not be too precious about keeping this workbook tidy or neatly compartmentalised, unless that is a powerful need for you. Allow it to be playful. Make doodles, sketches and draw your important dreams. Use the journal for newspaper cuttings too, so that all the material is together when you want to review your thoughts. This book is tangible evidence of the meeting point of your creative and

analytical thinking. The juxtapositions of happy accidents of chance can provide the 'Eureka!' that you were looking for.

Must I be selfish?

No. Discovering who you are and what would bring you a sense of prosperity does not mean you have to renege on all obligations and commitments. Knowing what would bring you joy can increase your prosperity, even if it is only a matter of adding another activity in a peripheral way. It may be that you will want to follow your creativity more wholeheartedly, after weighing up all the practical and instinctual elements. If this is so, others can only benefit from your increased contentment and the greater prosperity likely to flow from doing what most motivates you.

Ask for advice

It can help to ask several people who know you well, ideally in different capacities, to say what they consider to be your strengths and weaknesses. What do they see as your greatest talent? Ask people who you think will give a truthful answer. Flattery will not be of any practical use and may mislead you. Spitefulness may discourage you unfairly. Sometimes this task is more easily accomplished by those who have no emotional involvement with you, and for whom the prospect of your changing is no threat.

Research your interest

It is as important to make sound plans as it was to discover your real desires. If your interest would truly fulfil a dream, you probably already have background knowledge. In all likelihood you will always have noticed when information came your way, however

unlikely you thought its relevance to your situation. It is possible, however, that you so denied fulfilment of your creative needs that you must now research from scratch. In either case, you must become as well informed as you can. Your intuition needs the basic material to work upon.

- Is there a professional body concerned with the activity you would like to practise? A letter asking for details, contacts, addresses, classes, (if courteously accompanied by a stamped, self-addressed envelope) could get you started.
- Is there a publication which specifically deals with the subject area you are interested in? Not only do these have articles to keep you updated but they will also have the advertisements and contact information you need. There are specialist publications for more topics than you could dream of. A public library reference department will help you with this research. There are reference books listing every periodical and newspaper in print. There are specialist libraries such as that of the British Museum which hold stocks of every copy of every publication. Once you have seen a copy of the publication and assured yourself of its relevance, you may decide to take out a subscription, or alternatively find out where you can consult issues regularly.
- There are libraries which specialise in specific subject areas, some open to the general public, some for private use by members or employees. Most will respond favourably to a reasonable letter for assistance, again if accompanied by a stamped self-addressed envelope.
- Do you have access to the Internet, or information superhighway? Some libraries now offer access if you do not have the means at home.
- Perhaps further education is needed, or maybe you need to get practical experience such as getting a driver's licence or a teaching certificate. It is never too late to start. Opportunities might come your way long before you reach the end of the many years of training you imagine to be essential at the outset, but you need to be on the way to know about them. Take each step as it comes without worrying about a clear view of the final outcome. You are doing something that you have chosen for yourself, so

however long it takes, it should not be too hard to stay motivated. Beware of old patterns of negative thinking, but be realistic.

- Do not be put off entirely at the prospect of paper qualifications if you are daunted by them, unless your desired career path demands accreditation. Education is valuable, but enthusiasm and commitment can be more important to a shrewd employer, and irrelevant if you are setting up your own business. Some of the wealthiest computer barons today entered the field by being obsessive computer game enthusiasts and talented amateur programmers.

- Remember, the only real barriers that exist, are the barriers you erect in your own mind, so do not be completely intimidated by a company's formal employment strategy. A bit of flair, initiative and persistence in the right quarters can by-pass formalities. I was once successful in a job application because I kept applying every time there was an advertised vacancy and at regular intervals in between. By remaining enthusiastic, positive and respectful I was eventually interviewed and hired, with the comment that, 'You seemed so keen we decided we had no choice but to see you.' If you try this approach, judge the frequency of your applications with tact; often enough to be remembered, but not so often that you become a nuisance. Apply where it can have effect, to the head of personnel or recruitment, ideally by name. A call to the company switchboard can elicit this information without the likelihood of the enquiry arousing particular interest. Ask about the spelling of the name if it is unusual, a mistake of that kind is disrespectful and unlikely to meet with success. If you send applications without naming the intended recipient, you risk failure simply because it is never seen by anyone with enough authority to break with normal procedures. Do not waste all that flair! Company recruitment policies leave clerks little scope to deal with unorthodox applications. Be sure of your reasons for wanting this job, and what you have to offer, be courteous, but be determined.

- Is your intended activity one at which you could gain experience in a part-time or voluntary capacity while still maintaining your income in another way? Doing it is the thing, even if it takes lesser goals on the way to the main one.

Make sure you know what is involved to practise the kind of work or activity you have decided will bring you contentment. There is an infinite number of occupations available in the marketplace. Take a look at the business section of the telephone directory some day if you doubt this, and then multiply that by all the regions in your own country and abroad.

It may be that you have a satisfactory career but need to develop your leisure activities to achieve harmony and prosperity. Many of the techniques suggested on pp. 43–4 can equally well be applied to discovering how and where you can practise the activity you would like to add into your life. Could it be that you need to be as methodical about including holiday breaks as you are about that job that you are so good at? Your health and prosperity can only benefit from respecting and honouring your emotional and bodily needs. A sense of prosperity will come from doing what you truly love, in ways you simply cannot foretell, so do not make prosperity itself the goal, whatever aspect you choose to enhance.

flexible attitudes

Remember that success with lesser goals within the same subject will still be more rewarding than activity which has no personal meaning for you. Once again, you can never predict where or when opportunity may present itself, so do not dismiss small progressions by being obsessed with the major goal. Even prime ministers and presidents had to put in the work at lower levels on their way up. If you are not in the picture at all you cannot be noticed.

It would be sensible to think of various ways that the quality of experience you seek can be met in case the specific goal is not available to you at the present time. For example, if you have a deep-seated desire to act, and reason to believe in your ability to do so, there are various professions that exercise this quality, given that there are always more actors than parts at any given time. Could you perhaps lecture? There is quite a theatrical component to standing up before a class. Alternatively, maybe you could work as a

guide for a tourist attraction or holiday tour company. It would not necessitate giving up on the primary goal, the stage, but would serve to acknowledge your need to perform while providing a more satisfying source of income than other occupations would for you.

fast Lane or slow?

Do you want your change to prosperity to be dramatic, or would you be more comfortable with gradual change? The answer to this question will be unique and determined by your attitude to risk, and the needs of others who have to depend upon you. Prosperous people know what they want, and use their energies with focus and purpose. Do not splutter and misfire, scattering your energies to no purpose. Know yourself. Do you need to spend less or earn more? Perhaps you merely need to award yourself more holidays than has been your habit. Volunteer work can be a refreshing change and offer a different perspective, as well as benefiting others less fortunate than yourself. Might you be happier if you relocated? Would your life be improved if you were nearer to, or more distant from, your relatives? Are you at heart a town or country dweller? Did you always want a dog? Perhaps you always wanted to learn to fly? What area of your life do you see as a problem? What might you do to change the situation for the better?

Money, money, money

There is no escaping a realistic look at what you will be starting with. What is your present financial situation?

- Make complete lists of your assets, income and overheads. Take the trouble to be accurate, however tedious the task. Dig out the old bills. Ring the service company if you cannot remember what you last paid, if you did not keep copies. Ask what your bills have been over the last year or two so that you can assess an annual figure that allows for seasonal fluctuations.

- Are you living within your means at the moment? List your assets and liabilities to find out.
- Do you have a contingency plan to cope with enforced change due to bereavement, redundancy or ill health?
- Do you need to incorporate more relaxation and recreation into your life? How would you ideally like to do this? Make a start by gathering information about the hobby, sport or artistic endeavour that appeals to you and where you might pursue it.
- Debt does not go away by ignoring it. Can you reschedule your debts to one loan at a more favourable interest rate than many separate debts? What is the amount of your debt? Do you feel in control or do you need to seek professional help? This act alone may greatly increase your sense of prosperity, especially if you have been feeling trapped and too scared to assess your true situation.
- See if your council offers a debt advisory service. Ask your local Citizen's Advice Bureau. They often have specialists dealing with these matters on their behalf. You are far from alone in this problem and need not feel ashamed. If you have legal complications there may be a free law centre in your area. Find out what services are available. Debt is now such a widespread problem that many organisations are geared up to help, and they do so without censure.
- There are financial advisors who will help with investments and pension plans. Some do so free of charge. Check before you make an appointment what the fee situation will be. They want your business and are there to serve you, so do not be pressurised into taking the first one you contact. If you receive unsolicited offers of help from advisors, be wary. Check their credentials especially carefully. Maintain control. Ring several advisors if you find it difficult to refuse face to face, or take a friend with you. You do not need to add to your problems with expensive advisors when free alternatives exist. Check the telephone directories, your local reference library or Citizen's Advice Bureau, and the governing body of independent advisors.

Advisors should make their status clear. Independent advisors scan the whole financial sector and suggest whichever plan is best

tailored to the needs of the client, not just the products of one group who pay their salary. Some independent advisors take little or no fee from clients for the advice they give. They are paid commission by the companies whose products they successfully recommend. There may still be some bias according to where the commission is greater, but they should be willing to tell you the commission attached to each offer. By volume sales they may offer a better deal than you could get alone. You have a right to know commissions and charges if they are to be deducted from your investments. Get any advice you are given in writing and get a second opinion.

- What are the financial demands upon your income which must still be met if you attempt a new endeavour? Know how much must you earn to keep the present situation viable. Banks will give advice on the viability of projected new businesses, if you have prepared a clear plan and are aware of your overheads. They may be able to suggest grants to which you are entitled that will help to get you started.

- Know your weaknesses and strengths. If you know that you are a spontaneous spender you may need to set up controls to ensure that essentials are covered before you get your hands on 'silly money'. If you find it hard to anticipate cash flow for peak times, such as the winter bills, perhaps a budget account is the solution. With these, the bank settles all your bills as they arrive provided you pay them a set amount every month. This method frees you from clusters of bills all at once, followed by periods when there are none, when you might be tempted to overspend. The evened-out monthly amount is agreed between you and the bank after considering all annual overheads including contingency money for birthdays, Christmas and holidays.

- If on the other hand, you are a methodically cautious saver you may need encouragement to place some savings at risk in order to realise your dreams. This need not threaten your financial survival or mean total loss of control. Maybe you need to work on rewarding yourself and learn to enjoy the fruits of your labour.

- Do you have long-term goals? Do you know what you want for yourself at the age of 30, 40, 50, 60?

- Perhaps you are prepared to restructure your whole lifestyle rather than incorporate the demands of your present situation when moving towards your prosperous life? Be completely honest with yourself, as the only person you deceive and disappoint will be yourself.
- Refer back to the qualities which you now know to be personally important to your sense of well-being. If security is high on that list, then placing those familiar elements which give you a sense of identity and security at risk will inevitably compromise the success of what you risk them for. If bravado is not your style do not imitate it. Prosperity hinges on being who *you* are.
- Could it be that you do not need to earn more, but rather, spend less? It can be expensive to keep up a competitive lifestyle. Perhaps you would feel more prosperous with a lower income and less stress. Take other family members into consideration when considering down-sizing. You will need their co-operation and support as their lives will be affected.
- The qualities that you know are most important to you need not prevent you from aiming to reach goals that stretch your comfort zones a bit. By definition, the pushing of frontiers goes with breaking new ground. If you are making your own decisions for the first time, that can be scary. Be aware of how the steps you propose to take feel in advance. You can use creative imagination to sample new territory to some extent. Be aware, however, that what you cannot imagine may be just what will catch you out. Be ready to slip, learn, dust yourself off and start again. As an adult, mistakes need not engulf you. You may make mistakes but you will survive. Life is to be lived not feared, so be brave, have consideration for others, set up safety nets, then jump.

PRACTICE

1 Where would you research your chosen interest?
2 What caution is advisable when receiving financial advice?
3 What is the value of a flexible approach to the big goal?
4 How can less prove to be more?

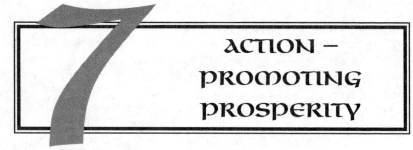

ACTION – PROMOTING PROSPERITY

Nothing great was ever achieved without enthusiasm

Ralph Waldo Emerson (1803–82)

L *ife can never be planned, covering all contingencies and anticipating all outcomes, from the security of an armchair. That much is obvious, though we often work ourselves into a frenzy of anxious planning as if it could. We must have goals and make a start if we are to fulfil our dreams and experience prosperity. It is essentially an active process. Have the goal, empower it with emotion and reason, then act.*

DETERMINING GOALS

I can think myself on the moon, but that alone would not put me there. That is true, but if I really held that long-term goal intensely enough, I would unconsciously steer my short-term goals towards an alignment with the interest I hold so passionately. To explain, I will take this extremely hypothetical case further.

WALKING ON THE MOON

If space were my passion, no doubt I would pay special attention in science and mathematics classes at school. I would be likely to read everything I could lay my hands on which touched on my subject,

from comics, through fiction, to textbooks. If I could not buy them or have them given to me, I would obtain them through the public library system. We are talking obsession, here.

It is possible for me to take classes that would eventually provide the necessary skills, learning and experience that are required of individuals picked for the space programme. Sure, it would take many years of dedicated study, and I might need to win scholarships, but if it is truly a passion, the motivation to persevere would be available, because this goal is who I am. I might need to pursue my studies abroad, if the technical expertise was not available at home, but that would just be part of my adventure. The big goal will be realised only by a series of small steps. The thing is, to begin!

You might ask what good it would do to become an astrophysicist or astronaut if no one is going to the moon any more. I agree that I cannot know when or if governments will spend money on space research, but if walking on the moon is really my passion, my effort will not have been pointless, and I guarantee it will bring me a sense of prosperity. How? Regardless of whether I ever step on to the moon or not, I will have spent my life immersed in the subject that I love. The rewards from that are unquantifiable, but here are some: given enough effort and application I will have a career in some way connected to this passion, and perhaps become an acknowledged expert in my field; I may work in a science laboratory or as a lecturer or teacher; I could become a technical advisor or a writer of scientific papers and books, or become a writer of science fiction. I might even join the staff at NASA, where at some future date space exploration may again be given government funding. There are many ways I could be near to the subject that I love. Whatever the future holds, I will have spent time and effort in the pursuit of what holds the deepest personal meaning for me, and the rewards, both financial and emotional, will positively affect all aspects of my experience. This is true prosperity. This principle applies universally, whether I long to drive moonbuggies or dustcarts, write sonnets or heal the sick.

Walking on the moon

What it takes is an awareness of our deepest desires and the courage to trust in them, and bring them into our life. We must determine what our goals are, if they are to be brought about. Determine *our* goals; not our parents' or educators' or neighbourhood goals. Many of the beliefs that we acquire while growing up are not appropriate for our adult needs or are just plainly untrue. If examined critically, they will be found to be counterproductive for our personally selected goals.

Get started

Your journey begins with the first step, so to reach the big goal you must overcome inertia and start with a small goal. In discovering what *you* truly want, you will have taken it. Your ultimate goal can seem somewhat abstract and unrealisable from your starting point,

so it is more effective to put your full energy and willpower into a succession of clearly defined stages on the way to the long-term goal, which you hold in mind at all times. You gain a sense of accomplishment with each step, and learn from any setbacks, without having risked all at once. As soon as you achieve one step, be ready to start work towards the next. If you allow complacency to creep in you can backslide to your old habits and position in no time. If you remain unsure of your ultimate goal because of long years of unquestioned acceptance, do not worry. In recognising the need to question, you have started the process that will reveal it to you, and that is the first of the smaller steps towards determining and successfully achieving your goal.

CREATING ABUNDANCE:
A FOCUSED WILL

Prosperity will flow when a focused, creative life brings together your efforts and desires. You have taken the time to consider what work would bring you the most satisfaction, if there were no barriers to your being able to perform it. Now you know the nature of your ideal work, or form of expression, and know what would make you feel prosperous. You also know your practical situation and have taken steps to organise and control your finances. You may have found that it is not the nature of your work which needs attention, but that you are too stressed and need to learn to make yourself the focus of relaxation, rather than aim for any external goal. Perhaps this is the time to arrange for a painting holiday on a Greek island or to pamper yourself with some aromatherapy sessions. It may be appropriate to consult a counsellor for help with deep seated problems. There should be no more stigma attached to recognising the need for this sort of help, than in recognising that few of us can fix damaged water or gas pipes without the aid of a professional.

The next step is to introduce into your regular relaxed sessions the picture of yourself already living the lifestyle you choose, in every

detail. Do not be shy or half-hearted about it. This is what you know would bring you a sense of prosperity, so this is no time for fear, doubt or indecision.

- See rave reviews of your West End stage performance.
- See yourself opening the latest of your many stores.
- Collect an Oscar for your latest film to add to those you already have.
- Accept the Booker prize for literature for your critically praised novel, currently top of the bestseller lists.
- Hear the speeches in your honour detailing the work you did which led to the award of the Nobel peace prize you see yourself collecting.
- Read the press reports of your latest successful business venture, while relaxing in your second home.
- Walk around your exhibition at the National Portrait Gallery and contemplate your new commissions.
- Accept a degree from Oxford University for your scientific success.
- Take that walk on the moon.

A WORD OF CAUTION

Remember, you cannot create anything that you have not first considered or imagined, whether that be an omelette, a work of art, or becoming prosperous in the way best suited to you. You will be taking practical steps, too, but the focused thought must be there first. I have been extravagant in my examples to emphasise the point. Be sure that you really would like life on a desert island before you pick too wild a fancy. If you might miss family and friends (this is not a package deal, their sense of prosperity might take them somewhere else entirely) and if you loathe insects, perhaps something closer to what you know would be more appropriate.

Be sure you really want what you ask for

PROSPERITY DAYDREAMING

The basic procedures are the same as for the self-assessment exercises.

- Make the daydreams as realistic as you can. This will help to weed out the impractical. Perhaps you have a desire to become a botanist or ecologist, and that desert island is just the place, but first mentally put yourself there, in a realistic setting and see how you feel about what you see there.
- Be exact about what you would be doing, with whom, where and how you would live. Be as specific as you can. Imagine your daily activities, the pleasures and difficulties. Put yourself fully into your idealised role. Follow a day through from beginning to end. How does it feel?
- If you experience fear or discomfort as well as pleasure, re-examine the chapter on resistance to prosperity, and ways to deal with

fears associated with taking responsibility for your prosperous life. By placing yourself imaginatively in your ideal situation you may be able to free yourself of these fears, by an examination of what triggers them.

- Keep reassessing and be honest with yourself. Does the fantasy still appeal as much when you have sampled it? It is better to realise that you were mistaken than to throw yourself into a life for which you are not suited. Be willing to reappraise if the taste is not as sweet as you had expected. You may by now have a more realistic idea of what is most likely to encourage your sense of prosperity, or even find that you had prosperity all along. Whatever you do, do not force yourself into a wrong choice rather than be willing to revise your goals.

- Does your ideal excite your ambition even more when you picture yourself already achieving it? Then you are on the right track.

- Once you know your goal, apply yourself. Do the research, make the contacts, take advice, make plans and set up safety nets. Involve those who depend on you, they may make your winning team.

- Monitor and adjust plans as you progress. Use relaxation techniques to stay in touch with your feelings and affirmations to reprogramme your attitudes and build confidence.

TRY IT ON FOR SIZE

Perhaps a specific everyday example would help. Let us imagine that you have decided a change of employment would be a desirable step towards your sense of prosperity. You know what you would much prefer to be doing, but before you take any steps in this direction, spend several sessions visualising yourself as already successful in the new career. Imagine all aspects of the new role as if you were actually employed in that sphere already, and most importantly, see yourself as successful in it. See also the lifestyle that you are living in your new position. Move freely in the imagined environment and be aware that it is entirely appropriate for you. Use affirmations which support this goal on a regular daily basis.

Visualise evidence of your success, in whatever way is appropriate to the activity, with no false modesty. If you think small, you will create small results. See yourself as eventually reaping the harvest of this success as well as simply achieving it. See yourself selling your company shares to retire in the sun, or see the development of your scientific idea to the benefit of all humankind. Dare to be bold, even if, to date, you have had little or no experience of success. It is important that you do not stop at visualising the achievement, but also programme in the rewards. If you preset a lesser goal you predetermine the limits of your success. Take it further so that you do not plateau or fall back into failure because you specified a limited success. Think big!

What if I cannot visualise?

If you have memories, you do it already, but do not think of it as visualising. Peacefully recollect the image of a much beloved location. Because this is actually known to you it will be easier to place yourself there again, and imagine that you are experiencing the qualities that you find so pleasurable but do not recollect a particular past memory. Just take yourself in your mind to that location and be there now. Give yourself a little time. When you are experiencing the sense of being there, you are visualising. Now calmly take yourself out of that location and into the one you want to experience. A good time to practise visualising is just on awakening. Your thinking faculties are suspended during sleep so resistance to visualising, or doubt in your ability to visualise, will therefore be less intrusive. Everyone can do it, as you can confirm.

I cannot stress the power of your imagination too often. You can employ affirmative visualisation of the goals you have set yourself to increase your focus on the issues. If you imagine vividly enough your mind can be deceived into reacting as if you have had an experience as a fact, so it is important to keep your visualisation and affirmations positive. You can equally well programme yourself for failure as for success, if you are careless.

Affirmations

Affirmations are a valuable tool for promoting prosperity. Once you know what you want to change or enhance about your lifestyle you may wish to employ this well tested method of positive auto-suggestion to bring about the changes you seek. You may find where your negative thinking lies from the nature of the retorts which spring to mind when uttering these positive suggestions. This is helpful for weeding them out and challenging them. For example, if the affirmation *I am talented* produces the mental response *No you are not, you are hopeless* you might start with questioning where that negative self-belief came from, whose voice is it? Get to work on reprogramming a positive appraisal of yourself even if you cannot find where the negativity sprang from. Prosperity is created in the mind first of all. Create the positive.

I have provided a list of affirmations at the back of this book which you may like to try. Some address a lack of prosperity with the aim of reprogramming negative blocks, while others promote increased self-esteem. Feel free to adapt or add to these affirmations. Select only one or two at a time and work with them for at least a week. Speak your chosen affirmation out loud, putting your name into the sentence, as suggested below. For example: *I, [your name], am now willing to experience an abundant prosperity.* Say these words aloud to yourself in the mirror, and to others (but not if among strangers who might doubt your state of mind!). Say them as many times a day as you can.

Write down the affirmations you are currently working with and place them where you will see them many times a day: beside the kettle or on the back of the bathroom door, for instance. You may also want to record them on a cassette tape to play back in the car, or when relaxing. It is a good idea to make the affirmations your last thought before sleep, unless you are planning to encourage a particular dream in that way.

Remember, you can tailor your own affirmations but they must be couched in positive language, and be active rather than passive. Find what negative thought patterns you hold and turn them into their positive counterparts. What you suggest must also be possible.

PRACTICE

1 What are the important features of an affirmation?
2 Why must your visualisation not stop with success but include seeing the rewards you stand to gain too?
3 What exercises can you use to focus your will?
4 Can everyone use visualisation techniques?

8
FENG SHUI AND PROSPERITY

It may, perhaps, seem fanciful to Western minds that the siting of architecture, location of activities or arrangement of furniture could affect the degree of prosperity we enjoy, yet the increasing popularity of feng shui in the West, together with its honoured status in the East, make this tradition worthy of your consideration.

Feng shui is used by many to improve the flow of prosperity to home and workplace. I am not a trained feng shui consultant, yet by applying simple principles and procedures I experienced a swift resolution of problems which I cannot ascribe to any other cause. I, therefore, have respect, if not understanding, for feng shui in action. The description I shall give here will be cursory, because more is beyond the scope of this book. If you want to try feng shui for yourself, I recommend that you refer to *Feng Shui for beginners* (see 'Further Reading') or any of the many detailed works now available on the subject.

What is feng shui?

This ancient Chinese art is broadly based upon a primary principle of Taoism: the belief that there exists a flow of energy, (referred to as *ch'i*) in and around all things. (In Taoism there is but one essential force.) Feng shui aims to harmonise your environment by identifying the location of your activities and the physical interruptions presented to the flow of this energy. If you employ feng shui

principles to your area of work and your home you can align their structures and your activities with the natural flow of *ch'i*, the force which acts upon them.

WhO cAN USE fENG ShUI?

If you are really serious about checking the feng shui aspects of your home or business, you should employ a trained consultant who will examine the property and advise you. For a fee, the consultant will suggest how harmony may be improved in general or in a specific area of experience, such as prosperity. In China people in business pay great respect to such advice.

If you would like to try some simple principles yourself, there are numerous books and courses available which give tuition and advice. When I tried remedies suggested by Richard Craze in *Feng Shui for beginners* I was surprised how quickly aspects of my life which had seemed obstructed for many months improved. Coincidence? Perhaps, but if you would like to improve your prosperity you need venture little to try it, too.

fENG ShUI IN pRACTICE

You will need to know the position of the property you wish to assess in relation to the points of a Western-style compass. These points are related in feng shui to particular types of experience. You may notice that feng shui does not treat polar north as the primary direction, as is the norm in Western cultures. In feng shui south is treated as the cardinal focal point. You will need to know in which direction your property faces (i.e. in which direction the front door faces). What follows is a very simple guide to the basics of feng shui.

1 Richard Craze recommends the construction of a chart called a *pah kwa* (or great octagon) upon which eight areas of experience, called *enrichments* are entered, together with the compass point with which each experience is traditionally associated in feng shui

practice. The following is a list of the compass points and the areas of experience with which they are traditionally connected:

- south   prosperity and fame
- south-east   wealth and money
- east   wisdom and experience
- north-east   children and the family
- north   relationships
- north-west   new challenges, change
- west   pleasure and gratification
- south-west   peace and harmony

You may care to note that feng shui also distinguishes prosperity as a quality different from and superior to wealth and money.

2 You will need a ground plan of the property in question, showing compass points, rooms, access ways, doors and windows, and also a note of the functions usually carried out in each area, for example: study; bedroom; leisure area; kitchen. You can sketch this yourself if you do not have a ground plan.

3 The amateur feng shui practitioner then overlays the pah kwa of traditional points and attributes on to the ground plan of the area to be assessed. Expert practitioners would not be likely to need visual aids for their appraisal since these principles would be so well learned. Whether the practitioner is an expert who can visualise the pah kwa, or an amateur with a sketched template, the compass point for the south (as located on the great octagon) must be placed to face in the direction of the site's actual main aspect or entrance as shown on the ground plan. (The main aspect will be the primary access point, regardless of whether or not it is actually used as such.)

4 The physical and functional layout of the property can then be read by reference to the great octagon, using its directional attributes like the hands of a clock pointing to what is actually sited there in comparison with the template. (Remember, south is always aligned with the primary entrance of the property, regardless of the property's actual compass direction).

5 It will have become clear that the south face shown on the great octagon, now placed towards the primary access point on the ground plan, may reveal that it actually lies in a direction quite

different, for example, from the south-east. This would mean that the attributes wealth and money (associated with the south-east on the pah kwa) are located at the entrance to your property. Now if the building's entrance happens to have what is regarded as a poor outlook, in feng shui terms, (for example, a rubbish tip opposite) you could have an explanation for experiencing poor monetary performance. Similarly, you might have difficulty with relationships if the primary access faces north and a rubbish tip.

Remedies

Fortunately, feng shui is not merely about identifying problems. It also offers solutions, though again, these may challenge the sceptical Western mind. I can only suggest that you suspend disbelief and give them a try. The remedies, though strange to our way of thinking, are not difficult to obtain or apply (and they do stop short of pulling the house down!). Harmony and a free, steady flow of energy is the aim.

It may be necessary to change the use to which you put particular rooms. Plants may have to be placed strategically, colour schemes altered, or furniture rearranged. Mirrors and mobiles may be placed to ward off too much ch'i energy, or to deflect negative energy. With practice you will soon become instinctually aware when disharmony has been created by misplaced objects or furniture. Perhaps you have always been aware that you prefer to sit in a certain chair without questioning why. An examination of feng shui principles affecting its location may surprise you with a wisdom you had not suspected.

Feng shui can thus offer greater insight into the conditions which create feelings of comfort and well-being. Armed with such awareness you can then maximise them. Prosperity can similarly be enhanced. Learn where prosperity is currently cited in your home. Keep your financial records and activities confined to this area if feasible. Discover whether the energy flow is interrupted to this location, or if it runs too swiftly through to benefit you. Your feng shui advisor or reference book will show you the features which

indicate these problems. You can then make the changes which will improve its flow.

PROBLEM: LOCATION OF ACTIVITIES

It is important within the principles of feng shui which activities are performed where. If you are unaware of the likely flow of ch'i energy, you could unwittingly encourage a negative emphasis to the life experience associated with a particular part of the building. This may mean that a certain room, or even a part of a room, is not being used to its best advantage for the activity most suited to it. For example, it would not be helpful to find that due to the unalterable geography of your property, you have your area of wealth and money located in the bathroom where it may quite literally flow down the pan. The expedient of keeping the toilet lid down when not in use and the strategic placing of mirrored surfaces are examples of suggested simple remedies for that predicament.

PROBLEM: BLOCKED ENERGY

In other cases an evaluation will reveal physical blocks to the free flow of this vital force. Perhaps you have a rubbish tip immediately opposite your front door. This would be regarded as poor feng shui. However, there are ways to minimise the influence of such a negative aspect. Depending on your precise situation you should be able to add remedies which effectively block or deflect this energy back to source. Once such a flow of energy is corrected by the suggested procedures, you should notice a freeing of the life experience which is ascribed to the entrance of the affected home or workplace. In the instance of a blockage this would mean a noticeable increase in the area of experience revealed by the great octagon as located at the entrance. This might be prosperity, for example.

PROBLEM: LOST ENERGY

We should also consider the opposite situation, which can just as easily occur. Investigation of the feng shui prevailing may reveal that energy, ch'i, is able to flow too rapidly away from your building or individual room. This situation understandably needs a different treatment by means of the strategic placement of particular objects according to prescribed principles. It is possible, for example, to use a plant or mobile to act as an entanglement which will slow the energy down, or make it flow more smoothly. A mirror can be used to act as a deflector in the case of energy seeping away from your site. You should acquaint yourself with the remedies for such situations explained in feng shui teaching.

Does feng shui work?

Some sceptical clients who have tried feng shui, myself included, have experienced astounding results almost immediately. Perhaps we should hold an open mind and accept favourable results which arise, whether we judge them as caused by the feng shui or the products of pure coincidence. We accept that we are surrounded by telecommunication signals at all times yet rational doubts are challenged by the idea of the invisible force, ch'i. As faith is not a requirement for success using feng shui, the end result should be the same either way.

Parallels with homeopathy

The effectiveness of feng shui can, perhaps, be likened to homeopathy, the alternative medical treatment founded by Samuel Hahnemann early in the nineteenth century. Hahnemann used observation and experiment to discover the twin principles of *'like treats like'*, and the effectiveness of a *'minimum dose'*, to trigger the body's natural responses to disease. Homeopathic remedial doses are prepared by successive dilutions to a point where they become too minute to be traced by any tests known to present science, yet results from their use are frequently astounding, even when applied in experimental conditions intended to disprove their efficacy. Animals treated homeopathically, for example, cannot be accused of

a placebo effect (the desire to imagine themselves well when no active medicine has been given) yet they do improve in more cases than could statistically be pure chance. A horse is not able to recognise that the medicine it is being given is homeopathic rather than allopathic, yet results predicted by the homeopath occur with such regularity that few racing stables choose to ignore its benefits.

Perhaps the important fact is that with good practice, both homeopathy and feng shui can work when we need them to. Maybe we should leave rational explanations for a more subtle science of the future. Homeopathy and feng shui cannot be guaranteed as infallible, but neither can Western, or allopathic medicine. Much of Western medicine works for reasons we do not understand either. All three disciplines are only as good as their practitioners, but that they can work is clear. So, why not try feng shui to increase your receptivity to prosperity? Its basic principles can be practised by a lay person and you have nothing to lose but your prejudice.

PRACTICE

1 What is the great octagon, or pah kwa ?
2 What is the primary compass point on the feng shui great octagon?
3 How might you deflect negative energy from entering your property?
4 If you wanted to increase your wealth, you might be advised to keep your financial records in your area of wealth and money. Where is this in your home?

BRINGING IT
ALL TOGETHER

Yesterday is dead, forget it;
Tomorrow does not exist, don't worry;
Today is here – Use it!

Wise words from a prosperous lady
nearing her hundredth birthday

*C**ore beliefs influence what is possible, so it is important to
become aware of acquired self-doubt and negativity and adapt
to a more positive approach. As we believe, so we receive. Of course,
we are not free to totally invent ourselves. We cannot decide to do
without air to breathe, nor can we manage unaided flight, however
dearly we hold such beliefs. There has to be recognition of the real
framework of our life, and the limitations within which we have the
scope to exercise our will. Prosperity, however, is a choice.*

You may ask what good a belief in prosperity would do someone
whose actual situation is just the opposite? I hope I have convinced
you that it is the first step towards realising whatever goals you hold.
Prosperity, like any other act of consciousness, involves focusing
your will productively.

The power of the focused will is our greatest gift. A life of imitation,
lived in second guessing what seems to work for others, is a life
wasted. Perhaps your own needs have been denied after years of

dutiful catering to the perceived needs of others? Through duty, fear or necessity we mimic other people's lives rather than choose to be responsible for our own. Placing others first is generally thought noble and altruistic, but if we do so only from fear and at the cost of ourselves, there may come a day of reckoning. Any extreme set of circumstances, perhaps the death of a loved one, divorce, separation, redundancy, or more pleasurably the birth of a child, or the winning of a fortune, can place intolerable stress on a borrowed life. Such enforced changes do, however, offer us the chance to re-evaluate. They are opportunities, even when the particular impetus is not one we would ever willingly have chosen.

Responsibility

Change need not be a recipe for rejecting all your ties and responsibilities. *Becoming Prosperous – a beginner's guide* is not a licence to be totally selfish, or self-centred. On the contrary, if we truly love others, they will be found to be a part of the desires that we uncover, when we allow our inner self to emerge. The relationship with loved ones will be found to be a part of who we are. When we take the time to know our deeper self we will realise just how firm that foundation is, rather than holding on to purely fear-based relationships: fear of losing approval; the need to secure the favour of those whose good opinion seems vital to our well-being; fear of our own anger; the effort to impress others or to gain, or maintain the acceptance of a particular group. All these stem from a lack of self-assurance and awareness.

If we doubt our own worth we live a pretence. We have a deep-seated fear that those whom we assume to have true worth will one day find us out, the game will be up, and we shall lose all the badges of wealth and status with which we have cloaked our insecurities. To take command of our own life and live in harmony with our deepest wishes makes for a happier, prosperous and more fulfilled individual, of much greater benefit to those with whom we

interact. Sadly, some people never take responsibility for their own happiness and die without ever knowing the satisfaction and prosperity which is available to them.

There is nothing fanciful about this approach to becoming prosperous. In the West we have tended to overvalue our analytical and rational capabilities to the detriment of our intuitive and creative capability. A prosperous individual is one who has learned how to value and utilise both. Each aspect of the mind then adds to and enhances the work of the other, if given the opportunity to function in its own way. The intuitive offers alternative solutions for the analytical to consider, but needs the raw material provided by the analytical to draw upon. True poverty is a life lived without personal fulfilment.

- Make consciousness a tool rather than the passive witness of events.
- Become aware of habitual, limiting thought patterns, and learn how to focus on prosperity as a conscious choice.
- Know your feelings and situation; then act.

Allow for change

Nothing in life remains static for long. Since these steps to prosperity are intended to promote change, it makes sense to be aware of the subtle shifts which occur, within and without. Stagnation denies prosperity because prosperity results from *living* a harmonious life, not from marking time on the way to the grave. By acquiring the habit of monitoring ourselves, we can maintain control, using the techniques of conscious appraisal and considered action. Our initial goals may never change, or we may find inner needs alter in the light of our ever-changing outer situation, and how we experience it. Do not expect what you want to come knocking at the door. Be active and start out for your goal now, even if you do have to make some changes on the way. Learn to choose your life rather than follow in its wake. Whose permission are you waiting for?

Ultimately, prosperity is a feeling of contentment and ease with what you have, and the knowledge that you are living in harmony with your creative nature. No one else's sense of prosperity will fit you, which is why hankering after what seems to please others is no way to find satisfaction yourself. When you make it a habit to listen to your inner needs and then utilise your present situation and skills to your best advantage, you will gain an unshakeable sense of prosperity because you will be exercising control over your own life.

Think prosperous

How you think controls the wealth and prosperity you will enjoy. Patterns of negativity effectively shun the prosperity which is already yours, so learn to recognise and change negative habits, and take control. If you resent others' wealth, how can you allow yourself to become one of them? You deny your prospects of experiencing wealth that way. Remember that people wedded to acquiring money do not feel prosperous anyway. Like rats in a treadmill they must chase after more and more, in a fruitless search for the satisfaction that will always elude them. Think positively about money as a neutral bearer of energy and do not block its flow. The more you are easy about giving, the more you are open to receive.

Think positively about yourself and your capabilities, and what activities you undertake. Think positively about those who may be of help to you and those who need your help. Learn to give your resources and yourself to others with love, and not from a sense of deprivation. Recognise what makes *you* happy and ignore what you assume gives happiness to others; you are probably quite mistaken. Enjoy the gift of your life.

PRACTICE

1 To be prosperous must you become selfish?
2 Why is it so important to believe in your right to prosperity?
3 Why should you continue to appraise your situation?
4 Are you ready for a prosperous life?

APPENDIX 1
AN EXERCISE IN
CREATIVE DAYDREAMING

Take some time to allow creative daydreaming. Nothing comes into being that has not been thought about first, so make some space for positive, focused thought.

Choose a time when you will not be interrupted. If you can manage twenty minutes or half an hour you will get more from this exercise, because it takes a few minutes for the usual mind chatter to settle down; all the, *what I did yesterday, what I must do tomorrow,* stuff. Even five minutes can be beneficial, and the more often you indulge in this mental massage and enjoy it, the more effective the time spent will be. The mind comes to know what is expected of it and quiets with less resistance.

It may help to visualise a favourite place, one you know or once knew, a place you would like to visit that you can visualise, or even an idealised place; pure fantasy. Take time to look about you. What can you smell, see, touch? Are you alone? Perhaps there are creatures or other people in the landscape? There is a seat nearby. Make yourself comfortable and feel the sunlight and a slight breeze upon your face. Bees are droning in nearby flowers and you can hear birds twittering in the hedgerow. This is a place that you can return to at any time you wish to relax.

Take a deep breath and relax all the stress from your body. If necessary, identify any physical tensions with these simple exercises, providing you have no medical conditions likely to be adversely affected by movement.

- Shrug your shoulders, raise them high and then drop them.
- Make fists of your hands and then relax them.
- Open your jaws wide and relax them.
- Flex your ankles then relax them.
- Slowly rotate your head on your shoulders.
- Take a deep breath and exhale slowly.

You are now ready to daydream about a specific issue. Iimagine yourself enacting one of your goals. Mentally place yourself in the situation you wish for and note how you feel as you do so. Discover what results develop in your daydream from this course of action. See the outcome and observe how you feel about it. If it feels rewarding, reinforce the idea by picturing yourself living this fantasy. Where would you be living? Would you have the same friends? Are you happy with the changes you imagine would flow from this course of action? Riches may impoverish if they separate you from the things and people you truly cherish. Be aware of any resistance or difficulties in the daydream, or in the attempt to daydream. Are you sure that you do want the goal that you are exploring? You may find that when viewed from this inner tranquillity this was not your own goal at all, that it was an aim you felt obliged to pursue to please others. Alternatively, perhaps you are still keen but foresee difficulties you had not previously considered. Maybe an utterly surprising topic comes to mind. Allow all possibilities to meander through your mind, however they twist and turn. Do not force their direction at this stage. In deep relaxation your instinctual self has a chance to slip through the limitations and barriers erected by your social self, so you may be surprised by what insists on claiming your attention, given this opportunity.

Remember the quiet place that you have created within yourself. You can return to it whenever you need to tap into your creative imagination.

APPENDIX 2
AFFIRMATIONS FOR A
PROSPEROUS LIFE

- I feel loved.
- I like myself.
- I can gain prosperity through doing what I enjoy most.
- I have talent which others will appreciate.
- I am safe and secure in all situations.
- My sense of prosperity does not depend on worldly wealth or success.
- I deserve prosperity.
- I am ready and willing to succeed.
- I am worthy of love whether I am prosperous or not.
- There is always enough time for what I really want to do.
- I do not fear disapproval.
- I am lovable.
- I can say 'No' without becoming unlovable.
- I accept that others may say 'No' without intending to reject me.
- I can initiate change without fear.
- I can create my own prosperity.
- My views are valid even if others do not share them.
- I accept that others have a right to hold views different from mine.
- I can be attractive and wealthy.
- I do not resent others' wealth.
- I accept and learn from all my life experiences.
- I am loved.
- I create prosperity in myself and others.
- The universe values and supports me.
- I enjoy my life.

- I can be prosperous and enjoy myself.
- I have an infinite amount of potential waiting to be realised.
- I am willing to accept success and money.
- The more I give others, the more I receive.

fURTḢER REAḊING

Bethards, Betty, *The Dream Book*, Inner Light Foundation, California, 1983

Cialdini, Robert B. *Influence: Science and Practice*, 3rd Edn. HarperCollins College Publishers, New York, 1993

Cooper, J. C. *An Illustrated Encyclopaedia of Traditional Symbols*, Thames & Hudson Ltd, London, 1982

Craze, Richard, *Feng Shui for beginners*, Hodder & Stoughton, 1994, and *Feng Shui – a complete guide*, Hodder & Stoughton, 1997

de Warren, Shaun, *You are the Key*, Wellspring Publications Ltd, London, 1988

Dyer, Dr Wayne W. *You'll see it when you believe it*, Arrow Books, London, 1989

Fromm, Erich, *The Art of Being*, Constable, London, 1993

Galbraith-Ryan, Lorna and Graessle, Lois, *Money's No Object*, Mandarin Paperbacks, London, 1991

Gregory, R. L. *Eye and Brain: The psychology of seeing*, 4th Edn. Weidenfeld and Nicolson, London, 1990

Holland, Ron G. *Turbo Success: How to Reprogram the Human Biocomputer*, Witherby & Co Ltd, London, 1993

Jennings, Marie, *Better money management*, Judy Piatkus Ltd, London, 1994

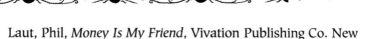

Laut, Phil, *Money Is My Friend*, Vivation Publishing Co. New Edition, Cincinnati, USA, 1990

Rogers, Brenda, *How to Solve Your Problems*, Sheldon Press, London, 1991

Todeschi, Kevin J. *The Encyclopedia of Symbolism*, A Perigree Book, New York, 1995

USEFUL ADDRESSES

UNITED KINGDOM

The Credit Counsellors Corporation (UK) Ltd
Buckingham House
Queen Street
London EC4R
Tel: 0800 363363

The Guild of Psychotherapists
47 Nelson Square
London SE1 0QA
Tel: 0181 947 0730
Central reference service to all areas

Investment Management Regulatory Organisation (IMRO)
Lloyds Chambers
1 Portsoken Street
London E1 8BT
Tel: 0171 390 6022

National Association of Citizens' Advice Bureaux
136–144, City Road
London EC1V
Tel: 0171 251 2000

Canada

Canadian Group Psychotherapy Association (CGPA)
11 Millstone Crescent
Whitley
ON LIR 174
Tel: 905/683 0099

Canadian Mental Health Association/
    Association Canadienne pour la Santé Mentale (CHMA)
2160 Yonge Street, 3rd Floor
Toronto
ON M4S 2Z3
Tel: 416 484 7750

Consumers' Association of Canada/
    Association des Consommateurs du Canada (CAC)
307 Gilmour Street
Ottowa
ON K2P 0P7
Tel: 613/238 2533

USA

American Counselling Association
5999 Stevenson Avenue
Alexandra V.A.22304

Chamber of Commerce of the USA
1615 H. Street N.W.
Washington D.C. 20062

Direct Marketing Association
W.42d Street
New York, N.Y. 10036–8096

International Consumer Credit Association
243 N. Lindbergh Boulevard
St. Louis MO 63141

National Association of College Admission Counsellors
1631 Prince Street
Alexandria V.A. 22314 2818

National Association of Investors Corporation
711W. Thirteen Mile Road
Madison Heights, M48071

National Business Education Association
1906 Association Drive
Reston, V.A. 22091

National Mental Health Association:
For referrals to mental health groups
Tel: 800 969 6642

Australia

The Australian Association of Somatic Psychotherapists
99 Queen Street
Ashfield
Sydney N.S.W.
Tel: 9716 6277

The Australian & N.Z. Society of Jungian Analysts & Psychotherapists
P.O. Box 190
Paddington
Sydney N.S.W.
Tel: 9360 6033

Australian Consumers' Association
57 Carrington Road
Marrickville
Sydney N.S.W.
Tel: 9577 3333

Business Enterprise Centres (N.S.W.) Ltd
382 Victoria Avenue
Chatswood
Tel: 9413 3230

Consumer Credit Legal Centre
24 Buckingham
Surrey Hills
Sydney N.S.W.
Tel: 9698 9448

Financial Planning Association of Australia Ltd
Canberra
Freecall 1800 337 301
Canberra State Executive Officer 293 4037

Financial Planning Association of Australia Ltd
Sydney N.S.W.
Freecall 1800 815 168
Sydney N.S.W. State Executive Officer 9299 8300

OTHER TITLES IN THIS SERIES

Astral Projection 0 340 67418 0 **£5.99** Is it possible for the soul to leave the body at will? In this book the traditional techniques used to achieve astral projection are described in a simple, practical way, and Out of the Body and Near Death Experiences are also explored.

Chakras 0 340 62082 X **£5.99** The body's energy centres, the chakras, can act as gateways to healing and increased self-knowledge. This book shows you how to work with chakras in safety and with confidence.

Chinese Horoscopes 0 340 64804 X **£5.99** In the Chinese system of horoscopes, the year of birth is all-important. *Chinese Horoscopes for beginners* tells you how to determine your own Chinese horoscope, what personality traits you are likely to have, and how your fortunes may fluctuate in years to come.

Dowsing 0 340 60882 X **£5.99** People all over the world have used dowsing since the earliest times. This book shows how to start dowsing – what to use, what to dowse, and what to expect when subtle energies are detected.

Dream Interpretation 0 340 60150 7 **£5.99** This fascinating introduction to the art and science of dream interpretation explains how to unravel the meaning behind dream images to interpret your own and other people's dreams.

Feng Shui 0 340 62079 X **£5.99** This beginner's guide to the ancient art of luck management will show you how to increase your good fortune and well-being by harmonising your environment with the natural energies of the earth.

Gems and Crystals 0 340 60883 8 **£5.99** For centuries gems and crystals have been used as an aid to healing and meditation. This guide tells you all you need to know about choosing, keeping and using stones to increase your personal awareness and improve your well-being.

The Goddess 0 340 68390 2 **£5.99** This book traces the development, demise and rebirth of the Goddess, looking at the worship of Her and retelling myths from all over the world.

Graphology 0 340 60625 8 **£5.99** Graphology, the science of interpreting handwriting to reveal personality, is now widely accepted and used throughout the world. This introduction will enable you to make a comprehensive analysis of your own and other people's handwriting to reveal the hidden self.

Herbs for Magic and Ritual 0 340 67415 6 **£4.99** This book looks at the well-known herbs and the stories attached to them. There is information on the use of herbs in essential oils and incense, and on their healing and magical qualities.

I Ching 0 340 62080 3 **£5.99** The roots of *I Ching* or the *Book of Changes* lie in the time of the feudal mandarin lords of China, but its traditional wisdom is still relevant today. Using the original poetry in its translated form, this introduction traces its history, survival and modern-day applications.

Interpreting Signs and Symbols 0 340 68827 0 **£5.99** The history of signs and symbols is traced in this book from their roots to the modern age. It also examines the way psychiatry uses symbolism, and the significance of doodles.

Love Signs 0 340 64805 8   £5.99   This is a practical introduction to the astrology of romantic relationships. It explains the different roles played by each of the planets, focusing particularly on the position of the Moon at the time of birth.

Meditation 0 340 64835 X   £5.99   This beginner's guide gives simple, clear instructions to enable you to start meditating and benefiting from this ancient mental discipline immediately. The text is illustrated throughout by full-colour photographs and line drawings.

Mediumship 0 340 68009 1   £5.99   Whether you want to become a medium yourself, or simply understand what mediumship is about, this book will give you the grounding to undertake a journey of discovery into the spirit realms.

Numerology 0 340 59551 5   £5.99   Despite being scientifically based, numerology requires no great mathematical talents to understand. This introduction gives you all the information you will need to understand the significance of numbers in your everyday life.

Pagan Gods for Today's Man 0 340 69130 1   £5.99   Looking at ancient gods and old stories, this guide explores the social and psychological issues affecting the role of men today. In these pages men of all ages and persuasions can find inspiration.

Paganism 0 340 67013 4   £5.99   Pagans are true Nature worshippers who celebrate the cycles of life. This guide describes pagan festivals and rituals and takes a detailed look at the many forms of paganism practised today.

Palmistry 0 340 59552 3   £5.99   Palmistry is the oldest form of character reading still in use. This illustrated guide shows you exactly what to look for and how to interpret what you find.

Qabalah 0 340 67339 7   £5.99   The Qabalah is an ancient Jewish system of spiritual knowledge centred on the Tree of Life. This guide explains how it can be used in meditation and visualisation, and links it to the chakras, yoga, colour therapy, crystals, Tarot and numerology.

Reincarnation and You 0 340 70517 5   £5.99   A practical guide to working with past and future lives, this book shows you how to improve this life, ease fear of death and make future lives better.

Runes 0 340 62081 1   £5.99   The power of the runes in healing and giving advice about relationships and life in general has been acknowledged since the time of the Vikings. This book shows how runes can be used in our technological age to increase personal awareness and stimulate individual growth.

Shamanism 0 340 68010 5   £5.99   Shamanic technique offers direct contact with Spirit, vivid self-knowledge and true kinship with plants, animals and the planet Earth. This book describes the shamanic way, the wisdom of the Medicine Wheel and power animals.

Spiritual Healing 0 340 67416 4   £5.99   All healing starts with self, and the Universal Power which makes this possible is available to everyone. In this book there are exercises, techniques and guidelines to follow which will enable you to heal yourself and others spiritually.

Star Signs 0 340 59553 1   £5.99   This detailed analysis looks at each of the star signs in turn and reveals how your star sign affects everything about you. This book shows you how to use this knowledge in your relationships and in everyday life.

Tantric Sexuality 0 340 68349 X   £5.99   Tantric Buddhists use sex as a pleasurable path to enlightenment. This guide offers a radically different and exciting new dimension to sex, explaining practical techniques in a clear and simple way.

Tarot 0 340 59550 7   £5.99   Tarot cards have been used for many centuries. This guide gives advice on which sort to buy, where to get them and how to use them. The emphasis is on using the cards positively, as a tool for gaining self-knowledge, while exploring present and future possibilities.

The Moon and You 0 340 64836 8   £5.99   The phase of the Moon when you were born radically affects your personality. This book looks at nine lunar types – how they live, love, work and play, and provides simple tables to find out the phase of your birth.

Visualisation 0 340 65495 3   £5.99   This introduction to visualisation, a form of self-hypnosis widely used by Buddhists, will show you how to practise the basic techniques – to relieve stress, improve your health and increase your sense of personal well-being.

Witchcraft 0 340 67014 2   £5.99   This guide to the ancient religion based on Nature worship answers many of the questions and uncovers the myths and misconceptions surrounding witchcraft. Mystical rituals and magic are explained and there is advice for the beginner on how to celebrate the Sabbats.

Working With Colour 0 340 67011 8   £5.99   Colour is the medicine of the future. This book explores the energy of each colour and its significance, gives advice on how colour can enhance our well-being, and gives ideas on using colour in the home and garden.

Your Psychic Powers 0 340 67417 2   £5.99   Are you psychic? This book will help you find out by encouraging you to look more deeply within yourself. Psychic phenomena such as precognitive dreams, out of body travels and visits from the dead are also discussed in this ideal stepping stone towards a more aware you.

To order this series

All books in this series are available from bookshops or, in case of difficulty, can be ordered direct from the publisher. Prices and availability subject to change without notice. Send your order with your name and address to : Hodder & Stoughton Ltd, Cash Sales Department, Bookpoint, 39 Milton Park, Abingdon, OXON, OX14 4TD, UK. If you have a credit card you may order by telephone – 01235 831700.

Please enclose a cheque or postal order made payable to Bookpoint Ltd, allow the following for postage and packing: UK & BFPO: £1.00 for the first book, 50p for the second book and 30p for each additional book ordered up to a maximum charge of £3.00. OVERSEAS & EIRE: £2.00 for the first book, £1.00 for the second book and 50p for each additional book.

For sales in the following countries please contact:
UNITED STATES: Trafalgar Square (Vermont), Tel: 800 423 4525 (toll-free)
CANADA: General Publishing (Ontario), Tel: 445 3333
AUSTRALIA: Hodder & Stoughton (Sydney), Tel: 02 638 5299